YESTERDAY'S SHREWSBURY

DAVID TRUMPER

SUTTON PUBLISHING

Sutton Publishing Limited
Phoenix Mill · Thrupp · Stroud
Gloucestershire · GL5 2BU

First published 2002

Title page photograph: Barker Street, *c.* 1955.
Front endpaper: Abbey Foregate, 1964.
Back endpaper: Children tempted by Alan and
Dorothy Reynolds's sweet selection, 1950.

British Library Cataloguing in Publication Data
A catalogue record for this book is available from the
British Library.

ISBN 0-7509-2921-9

Typeset in 10.5/13.5 Photina.
Typesetting and origination by
Sutton Publishing Limited.
Printed and bound in England by
J.H. Haynes & Co. Ltd, Sparkford.

Shrewsbury, *c.* 1960. Anthony Hector took this wonderful aerial view of the town. It shows how Shrewsbury is almost completely encircled by the Severn, except for a narrow piece of land to the north, which was successfully protected by the castle. The Welsh Bridge can be seen on the left and the English Bridge on the right. The old cattle market on Smithfield Road, the Market Hall at the top of Mardol and the Shirehall in the Square are still prominent features as is the new Telephone Exchange on Town Walls. The poet Leland was very impressed with the town: 'Built on a hill fair Salop greets the eye,/While Severn forms a crescent gliding by./Two bridges cross the navigable stream./And British Alders gave the town its name.' (*A. Hector*)

CONTENTS

Harlescott, *c*. 1960. The Glasgow firm of Alley & MacLellan moved their factory to Shrewsbury in 1915. They bought 16 acres of land on the west side of the Whitchurch Road and within four months the first wagons were rolling off the assembly line. The factory was known as the Sentinel Waggon Works until 1957 when Rolls-Royce bought them. This photograph was taken during one of their open days when people would queue to be shown around the works. Inspecting the entry tickets outside the main office block is ex-Police Constable Horace Boulton, the security guard. Above the man with the coat over his arm is the famous Sentinel statue, whose motto was 'Ever watchful, on the alert'. (*Author's Collection*)

INTRODUCTION

The selection of photographs in this book depicts life in Shrewsbury, as it was in the 1950s and '60s, and are chosen mainly from the hundreds of views of the town taken in 1960 that are now preserved by Abbeycolor. The Herculean task of photographing every shop front and street in Shrewsbury was undertaken by Bernard and Bill Cross who owned W.G. Cross & Sons, a photography shop in Mardol.

Around 1,000 photographs were taken, mainly by Bernard Cross, and have proven to be a time capsule of images of how we lived at this period. It shows the town before the era of the supermarket and the large shopping centres when family firms still ruled the High Street. Names such as Maddox, Della Porta, Overy, Frank Newton, Hammonds, Wilding and Beddard all conjure up images of good quality and excellent service.

There are views of the Raven, Crown and George Hotels and the public buildings such as the Shirehall, Post Office and Market Hall, all torn down in the 1960s in the name of progress. The photographs also show the awful conditions that still survived in some areas of the town where people lived in back-to-back housing with no indoor sanitation or running water. Although many of these scenes have disappeared, they are still preserved in these wonderful black and white images, which evoke so many memories.

Not satisfied with preserving images of the town in 1960 the brothers repeated the operation in 1980, but this time in colour. In the summer of 1999, at the age of seventy-eight, Bernard Cross undertook the enormous task again photographing the whole of Shrewsbury, presenting them to the Shropshire Records and Research Centre for safe keeping. Like the 1960 photographs, those taken in 1980 and 1999 will be a wonderful source of information for future historians of the town.

This book also contains photographs by four keen amateur photographers who had the foresight to capture views of the town that stimulated their interest and to preserve them for posterity. Antony Hector combined his interest in flying to capture a number of photographs of the town from the air. He also took many street scenes in the 1950s that were made into postcards that capture perfectly the style and the atmosphere of that era. David Mitchell, who ran the electrical firm of A.R. Mitchell in Mardol, took many publicity photographs for his business and of events that hired out their public address systems. Another Mardol businessman, H.R. 'Jim' Savage, who owned the grocery business of R. Goodwin & Co., was a prolific photographer. Between 1920 and 1985 he took 1,000s of images of the town and of the changes that occurred during that time. The fourth photographer to feature in this edition is John Bumford, a local man who documented the many changes that affected the town in the late '50s and early '60s. Among the photographs he is responsible for are the interesting view of the building of the new Shirehall taken from the top of the column and the devastating fire that gutted the premises of A.D. Foulkes in Barker Street.

Managing Director Adrian Madin with the fully restored classic Fordson van, which reappeared for promotional purposes. Mr Madin's father-in-law Tony Brazier set up shop as a commercial photographer and a photo finisher, and founded the West Midland Photo Services Ltd in 1932 down Water Lane in New Street. The firm moved to its Frankwell premises and was eventually taken over by Mr Madin who entered the business in 1960. The company developed and expanded throughout the 1960s, '70s, and '80s, changing its name to Abbeycolor and moving into other fields, which included industrial, commercial, architectural and school photography, as well as a collection and delivery service for developing film for several Boots stores and other outlets in and around the county. The firm is now being managed by a third generation, Mr Madin's sons, Simon and Giles. (*Abbeycolor*)

1

Around the Square & High Street

The Square, *c*. 1960. The market was moved here from St Alkmund's Square in about 1272. The Plough Inn on the left was first mentioned in 1672 and is housed in part of a building once known as the Selds or Shields, a row of shops belonging to the drapers of Shrewsbury. An ancient shut or passage once ran to the side of the building, linking the Square with Mardol Head. The Square end is now enclosed in the Plough, while the Mardol Head end is open just to the rear of the inn. In the 1960s the landlord, Jack Keech, objected when they renamed the passage Plough Shut, as he thought it implied that his inn was closed. On the High Street side of the Square is Martins Bank in a timber-framed building known as Cartwright's Mansion. Next door is a very ornate building, built in the Flemish style for the Alliance Insurance Company in 1891 at a cost of £6,690. The architect was A.E. Lloyd Oswell of Dana Chambers. The Halifax Building Society now occupies the premises. The building to the right was occupied by the Midland Bank from 1901, when it was known as the North and South Wales Bank. The building that now houses Waterstones dates from 1713. For over fifty years the gentlemen's outfitters Ronald Beck traded from there, until the business closed in January 1988. (*Abbeycolor*)

The Square, *c.* 1960. Redmayne & Co. opened this business in about 1860. They also had shops at 20 Bond Street in London and at Harrogate in Yorkshire. By 1877 Millard Harding had become a partner in the firm and by 1881 had taken full control of the business. H.L. Grocott bought the business in the early 1890s. In 1936 the shop was purchased by Mr W.H. Lamb, who owned it until the business was amalgamated with Great Northern & Southern Stores, although it still traded under the name of Grocott until its closure in the mid-1960s. Throughout the first half of the twentieth century it was one of the most fashionable ladies' stores in town, with customers from all over the county. (*Abbeycolor*)

The Square, *c.* 1960. In the nineteenth century this shop was the Christian Knowledge & National Society's Depot. It became a grocery shop in about 1900 when it was run by Samuel Heighway and was taken over by Henry Lee in about 1915. In 1952 he was described as a 'Family Grocer of Quality'. His shop was privately owned, carried the most comprehensive stock in the county and would deliver to all parts of Shropshire and into mid-Wales. Personal attention, courtesy and consideration were assured. The shut to the right, which links the Square to College Hill, is known as Coffee House Passage, as an eighteenth-century coffee house was situated there. On the roof of the passage, just inside the entrance, is a tie beam with the initials GP and the date of 1577. (*Abbeycolor*)

The Square, *c.* 1970. This unusual view of the Market Hall was taken from Princess Street after the demolition of the Shirehall. The building was erected in less than a year and was opened in 1596. It is built out of Grinshill stone in the Renaissance style and is similar in appearance to the library buildings on Castle Street; it is likely to be the work of the same man, probably Walter Hancock. The ornamental parts of the building include the arms of Elizabeth I, a statue of the Duke of York, which was rescued from the old Welsh Bridge, an angel holding a shield bearing the arms of England and France, saved from one of the town gates, and a splendid sundial. The upper floor is supported by Doric columns with semi-circular arches. (*Abbeycolor*)

The Square, *c.* 1955. The Gullet Passage is one of the town's oldest shuts and connects the Square to Mardol. The origin of the name is unknown, but it has been suggested it comes from a medieval word, 'golate', meaning a channel or ditch, as once an open stream ran down the passage and Mardol, which drained a pool in the Square. An inn known as the Gullet once stood at the Mardol end on the site now occupied by the Market Vaults. It was there from the sixteenth century until about 1793. A deed of 1630 mentions that the inn possessed an enclosed court for real tennis, and throughout its history it seems to have been the meeting place for a number of bands of travelling actors. (*Author's Collection*)

Princess Street, *c*. 1960. In the nineteenth century this shop was a clothes store run by Francis Hood, but by 1905 had been taken over by Joseph Onions who was listed as a shopkeeper. Herbert Dann had a tobacconist and confectionery shop at 17 Princess Street, but after his death his wife moved the business to these premises; eventually it was taken over by Bert, his son. Bert was a popular and well-known character around the town in the middle part of the last century and is remembered for the dances he used to run at the Lion Hotel on a Saturday night. Bert would stand at the bottom of the stairs leading to the ballroom to collect your money on the way in and to stamp your hand if you needed to pay a visit to the cloakroom. Several hundred years ago a fire destroyed many buildings in this area and four young children were burned to death in this house; their spirits are reported to haunt the building. (*Abbeycolor*)

Princess Street, 1960. Bert Dann's shop was on the corner of College Hill and Princess Street and PDC Copyright, a printing firm, now occupies the building. Honeychurch's shop and showroom was next door; he was a cutler, toolmaker and ironmonger. Beyond Honeychurch's, Walker, Emberton & Co. have their soft furnishing shop. Part of that building was once a public house called the Bell. Records for the inn date back to 1658, and it was listed for nearly 300 years until it was delicensed in 1925. (*Author's Collection*)

Milk Street, 1960. Milk Street was once part of a road that ran from the end of High Street to Town Walls and was known first as St Chad's Lane, after the church, and then as Stury Close Lane, after a medieval family who owned land in the area. The ICI building on the left is built on the site of the Shearmen's Hall, which was demolished in about 1895. George Proud, a local draper who was Bailiff of Shrewsbury in 1568, built the timber-framed building next door. A descendant of the family married Ann Milton, the sister of John Milton the poet. (*Abbeycolor*)

The Old Post Office Hotel, *c.* 1955. The inn was first recorded in 1804 and occupies part of the mansion built by George Proud in 1568. For many years the landlord was Sam Powell, a well-known sporting figure in the town. He had links with Shrewsbury Town Football Club, ran a boxing club and a gymnasium and was involved with local athletics. The inn was often a venue for sporting committee meetings and the rooms were full of photographs of different sportsmen and sporting events. At one time there were twenty rooms at the hotel, thirteen private and seven public. Eleven of the private rooms were for the accommodation of twenty-two guests. (*Author's Collection*)

College Hill, 1960. The name of the street dates from about 1746 and refers to the college that was attached to old St Chad's Church, which was dissolved in 1541. In 1641 the street was known as Horton's Lane and for a short time in the eighteenth century as St Chad's Hill. G.H. Smallwood had his electrical business at 5 and 6 Milk Street until he moved his workshop and offices to these premises in the 1930s. At this time he also had a showroom at 13 High Street and branches at 5 Old Street, Ludlow, and 2 The Square, Church Stretton. He was listed as an electrical, radio, refrigerator and mechanical engineer. By the 1950s he had also expanded into television. In 1960 Cecil Smallwood sold his High Street shop to Broadmeads, bringing their number to 351 shops around the country and giving them a foothold in Shropshire. (*Abbeycolor*)

College Hill, 1960. The hill connects Princess Street to Swan Hill and contains some very grand houses. Lord Clive lived in the street when he was Mayor of Shrewsbury in 1762. The small timber-framed building on the right was a small veterinary practice, started by Arthur Curtis and taken over by Richard Parsonage in about 1930. The large building is the rear of the Music Hall and just beyond that is the Freemasons Hall, which contained parts of the ancient Vaughn's Mansion. At the bottom of the street in Swan Hill is a public house, which was first recorded in about 1835 as the Talbot Tap with links to the Talbot Hotel in Market Street. It became known as the Admiral Benbow in 1861, commemorating a gallant Shrewsbury citizen who has been called the Nelson of the seventeenth century. (*Abbeycolor*)

The Square, *c.* 1960. The Annual Electrical Homes Exhibition was held at the Music Hall between Tuesday 27 and Friday 30 September, and was open daily from 11a.m. to 9p.m. with free admission. The show was organised by the Midland Electricity Board and the other leading electrical dealers in the town. It was advertised as having something for all the family and was well attended by the public. The organisers also boasted that it was 'Packed with every possible aid to better, easier, cheaper living'. You could see the kitchen of tomorrow, all the up-to-date television sets ranging from 50 to 100 guineas and the latest radios and record players for the youngsters. The leading firms at the show were A.E. Jones (Electric) Ltd, Medlicott Bros, H.F. Pollard (Shrewsbury) Ltd, and A.R. Mitchell (Shrewsbury) Ltd whose stand we see in this photograph. (*D. Mitchell*)

The junction of Market Street and Swan Hill, 1956. Market Street was originally known as Cornechepingstrete or Chepingstrete. Cheping is derived from the old word 'ceap', which denotes a market. In 1956 this building, known as Talbot Chambers, was up for sale. It had once been a hotel, where the young Princess Victoria and her mother, the Duchess of Kent, stayed when they visited the town in 1832. The shops occupying the ground floor were, from the far end, Little & Cooper, leatherwear and travel goods retailers; Affords (Dry Cleaners) Ltd; Healthiway Stores, 'nature food' retailers; E.W. Bridgwood, gents' outfitter, and on the corner the Shrewsbury Café Co. Ltd, retail confectioners and restaurant who traded under the name of the County Café. The upper storeys were occupied as offices. The building was gutted by fire on 12 February 1985 and the Lloyds TSB bank now occupies the site. (*Author's Collection*)

Mardol Head and Pride Hill, 1960. Until the middle of the nineteenth century the timber frame of Lloyds Bank was hidden under a coat of plaster. The frontage was uncovered and greatly restored when the bank took the building over in about 1876. When the building was modernised in the 1960s planners had hoped to keep the old front, but owing to building difficulties the plan was dropped, and a modern version of a jettied building was adopted instead. Known as 'The Fifty Shilling Tailor', John Collier opened his first shop in Shrewsbury on Pride Hill in July 1929. The shop was remodelled in 1962 to include the remains of Benet's Hall, which dates from the thirteenth century. Hilton's shoe shop opened in these premises after moving from Mardol at the beginning of the twentieth century. The shop finally closed in 2001. (*Abbeycolor*)

High Street, 1960. The large timber-framed building on the left is Ireland's Mansion. Robert Ireland, a wealthy wool merchant, came from Oswestry and was Bailiff of Shrewsbury in 1566 and again in 1579. The building was later converted into three separate premises. S.N. Cooke, a ladies' outfitter and haberdasher, occupied the left-hand side of the building. The shop in the centre belonged to John Adams, a chemist, and when it moved to Market Street the premises were occupied by an electrical shop run by John James, who had a marvellous record department in the basement. The end section was for many years the Westminster Bank. Owen's Mansion and Cartwright's Mansion are on the right. (*Abbeycolor*)

High Street, 1960. The North and South Wales Bank opened a branch at 20 High Street in July 1901. In 1908 the bank amalgamated with the London City and Midland Bank, which later became known as the Midland Bank. The company moved sites in about 1973 into the new Princess House just across the road. The bank is now known as the HSBC. Ronald Beck opened his gentlemen's outfitters in 1932, taking over the premises of Donald Wells, the jeweller. He traded there until January 1988 and was well known for the quality of his goods and his unusual adverts, written in a very distinctive hand. H.E. Randle sold boots and shoes, while Murrell's, who had traded in the town for well over a hundred years, sold all your garden needs. They also had a large garden centre at Portland Nurseries, where they invited customers to view the acres of young rose trees and receive free advice on the most suitable for their garden. Bradley's on the other corner of Grope Lane moved to this site from Pride Hill in 1939. They were a Chester firm and they took over the business of Thomas Golling, the tie expert. Foster Brothers in turn bought them out. (*Abbeycolor*)

The large department store of Della Porta celebrated its centenary in May 1957. It was founded in a very modest way by Joseph Della Porta who had arrived in England from Italy in 1848. He opened as a general dealer in a small shop in Princess Street, but in a short time had expanded into 1 to 5 Princess Street and around the corner into Lloyds Mansion in the Square. By the 1930s the County Council were looking to extend the Shirehall on to the Lloyds Mansion site, which gave Della Porta an opportunity to purchase land on High Street, immediately in front of his Princess Street premises, and link the two. This magnificent frontage was erected to blend in with the Shrewsbury image and a grand opening was held on 12 July 1933. Joseph William Della Porta, the grandson of the founder, was the last member of the family to take an active interest in the firm, which was eventually taken over by Rackhams. (*Abbeycolor*)

Grope Lane, *c*. 1960. The lane, which connects Fish Street to High Street, retains a great deal of its old medieval character. The name is often given to a dark, narrow alleyway through which you grope your way, and there are similar lanes in Oxford, York, Peterborough and Northampton. In the past it has also been known as Dark Lane and Boot Lane. The building on the left was once a public house called the Cross Keys. It was renovated in the 1980s and now bears the images of Margaret Thatcher and Mick Jagger carved into its ancient timbers. (*Author's Collection*)

2
Pride Hill
& Castle Street

The junction of Pride Hill, Castle Street and St Mary's Street, *c*. 1955. On the left is part of Morris's main shop, built in 1927 and modelled on Blickling Hall in Norfolk. Just beyond is the marvellous shop sign of F. Farmer, the optician, who is next door to A.L. Salisbury, the leather merchant. On the corner of Castle Street and St Mary's Street is Barclays Bank who rebuilt on that site in 1959. The cross was presented to the town by Shrewsbury School on the school's four hundredth anniversary in 1952. It is inscribed in Latin: 'The Royal School of Shrewsbury presents the cross to the town it loves. It changed its site but not its loyalty.'
(Author's Collection)

Pride Hill, 1955. The name of this street is taken from the Pride family who owned a mansion, a shop and land in the area from the thirteenth century. Before that the left-hand side of the street was occupied by a number of butchers and was known as the Shambles or Butchers' Row, while the other side was occupied by cobblers and was known as Corvisor's or Shoemakers' Row. Like Castle Street, Pride Hill has also been known as High Pavements or High Street. The chemist shop on the right belonged to E.J. Jones Ltd, while just below them was Masters & Co., the gentlemen's outfitters. E.A. Afford, another gentlemen's outfitters are in the white building. At first glance the elaborate ornamental frontage of that building looks like stucco, but it is in fact cast-iron and was made at the Coalbrookdale foundry for a Mr Biggs, a florist, and the designs depict his trade. In 2001 the frontage was tastefully renovated by Patch, the jewellers, when they moved their shop there. (*Abbeycolor*)

Pride Hill, 1960. This view of Pride Hill was taken after dark but the round light in the top left-hand corner is not a full moon but one of the four green illuminated dials of the Victorian Market Hall clock. Within twelve months of this photograph being taken most of the market and the whole of the clock tower would be demolished. In the five years from the previous view very little had changed. The Pipe Shop, the chemist, Affords, and Lyons café are still there but Master has been taken over by Weaver To Wearer. (*Abbeycolor*)

The rear of Pride Hill, *c.* 1960. This is a view of the lower part of the old town wall, taken from Raven Meadows. It was built in the middle of the thirteenth century, but in more peaceful times the top section was dismantled and the bottom section was used as the foundation for a town house. There is evidence of three phases of building on this site. The lower section shows the remains of a fourteenth-century structure, which is supported by stone buttresses from the sixteenth century and arcades built of brick from the eighteenth century. The stone extension to the left is the garderobe or medieval toilet, which discharged its waste into a channel in Raven Meadow. To the right of the building was a shut, a flight of thirty-one steps leading from Pride Hill into Raven Meadow. The bottom section, including the garderobe and the steps, has been incorporated into a McDonald's restaurant. (*Author's Collection*)

Pride Hill, 1960. Since this photograph was taken all the businesses on the left-hand side of the street have disappeared. The shoe shop known as Freeman, Hardy and Willis moved from here into Mardol, while Collier's was taken over by Richards when they moved down the road to their new store on the site of Benet's Hall. Harold Honeychurch, who was listed as a pastry cook, had a café and cake shop on this corner for around forty years. In the 1960s the building was rebuilt to house the Golden Egg Restaurant but has since been taken over by the travel agent Thomas Cook. The shop next door was the Singer Sewing Machine store for many years before C.M. Keenlyside opened his chemist shop there. Next to him was Lawleys (of Regent Street) Ltd, who sold glass and china, then Baker's jeweller's shop, and, in the timber-framed building, the tobacconist and pipe business belonging to Alfred Preedy & Sons. The shop was known locally as Pelican & Snelson's and part of that building dated back to the fifteenth century. The shop was sold in 1978 for £30,000 and is now occupied by Thornton's the confectioners. (*Abbeycolor*)

Pride Hill, *c.* 1963. Lyons Café and Tea Rooms was a favourite place to visit for the lady shoppers of Shrewsbury in the 1950s, when two sisters ran it. It was opened in the 1940s in an old hairdresser's shop belonging to Percy Shaw and it closed in the 1970s. Hudson Verity next door were opticians. They moved to a new row of shops in Barker Street and were taken over by Dollond & Aitchison. Note the new no waiting signs on the left. On 23 October 1963 the *Shrewsbury Advertiser* warned motorists about the town's strict new parking rules and to 'watch the yellow lines'. (*Abbeycolor*)

Pride Hill, 1960. Boots the Chemist came to Shrewsbury at the beginning of the twentieth century and were housed at 10 Mardol Head. This building was erected for them in 1902 and has been extended twice, in 1920 and again in the 1970s. The architect designed a timber-framed frontage, which was supposed to fit in with the local townscape; unfortunately he chose a design that would have looked more at home in Ipswich than Shrewsbury. During the 1930s the store had a beautiful café and tearoom, which could accommodate 200 people and had its own palm court orchestra. (*Abbeycolor*)

Pride Hill, 1960. Richard Maddox opened his first shop in Shrewsbury in Gloucester House on Castle Street in about 1842. In December 1862 he opened a new draper's shop at 26/7 High Street; in 1869 he extended his premises around the corner into Pride Hill; and he added a further four extensions in both Pride Hill and High Street before the end of the nineteenth century. Owen Owen took over the store in 1975. (*Abbeycolor*)

Pride Hill, 1960. F.W. Woolworth & Co. opened their 'Penny Bazaar' in the early 1930s. The shops it replaced were Bagnall & Blower, the grocers, and the Steward Brothers who were listed as provision merchants. Harry Steward had the distinction of being Mayor of Shrewsbury eight times between 1937 and 1945. Woolworth moved from here into Castle Street in 1964 and this store was sold to Timothy White's for £250,000. The buildings were demolished in the 1980s for the entrance to the new Darwin Shopping Centre. The family business started by Alfred Overy, to the right, celebrated its centenary in 1968. The shop specialised in men's and children's clothing and they had another branch in Bailey Street in Oswestry. The business was sold to Dunns. (*Abbeycolor*)

Castle Street, 1960. Scull Brothers, who were listed in 1964 as plumbers and sanitary and heating engineers, were founded in 1834 and have traded from 31 Castle Street for over a hundred years. Henry Fields was a ladies' outfitter, while Wildings sold a variety of goods from China and glassware to books and art material. They also had a wonderful record department in the basement, run for many years by Mrs Fox, whose knowledge of the record industry was unsurpassed. On offer for Christmas 1959 were 'Little Donkey' sung by Gracie Fields and priced at 6s, and 'Red River Rock' by Johnny and the Hurricanes at 6s 4d. The small timber-framed building that housed Groves jeweller's shop is an original sixteenth-century dwelling, while the larger one to the right is an oversized Victorian copy. (Abbeycolor)

The Co-op, Castle Street, c. 1960. The opening of Shrewsbury Co-operative Society's new Registered Office and Central Emporium took place at 3 a.m. on Wednesday 31 October 1923. It was carried out by the President of the Society, Mr W.F. Hunt, who thanked the committee for the honour they had conferred on him. He was assisted by the Mayor and Mayoress of Shrewsbury, Alderman and Mrs T. Pace, the Deputy Mayor and Mayoress, Alderman and Mrs Toye, the Mayor and Mayoress elect, Councillor and Mrs Bates Madison, and a crowd of several thousand people. The new building, designed by F.E.L. Harris, stood on the site of Thornes Mansion, and in his speech the Mayor thanked the architect and the society on the magnificent service they had rendered the town by the erection of such beautiful buildings. When the doors were unlocked the arcade and all the departments were filled to overflowing, and the café staff were swept off their feet in the rush. (Author's Collection)

Castle Street, 1960. Werfs ladies' outfitters occupied this corner shop from the early 1950s until quite recently, while to the right is the Scotch Wool & Hosiery Co. The District Bank, under the management of Mr G.C.C. Atkinson, opened this office in the town in 1935. By 1972 it had become a branch of the National Westminster Bank and extended into the photographic shop of R.G. Lewis. Modelia was a ladies' fashion shop, occupying Hammond's fish and poultry shop seen in the next photograph. Today the premises have been split into two units, one being occupied by Jessops. (*Abbeycolor*)

Castle Street, 1953. Frederick and Thomas Hammonds opened Hammonds' fish, game and poultry shop in the 1890s, although their father had been involved in the fish business since before the railway came to Shrewsbury, bringing fish covered in ice by horse and wagon from Birkenhead and Bangor. The Royal Warrant over the door shows that the shop once supplied Queen Victoria with fresh fish and game when she was staying at Bala as a guest of Sir Henry Robinson. The firm was taken over by Frederick's son Cecil, who installed the large window fridge in the early 1950s at a cost of £1,000. It was thought to be the first such fridge in the county. The Christmas display of poultry would now be frowned on by Health and Safety. (*Author's Collection*)

Newton's and Whitfield's shops, Castle Street, July 1960. Three generations of Newtons had run this gentlemen's outfitters. It was known throughout the town as 'The Big Hat', as it once had a huge top hat hanging outside as a shop sign. The hat was the size of two grown men standing shoulder to shoulder and was said to have been made from part of a consignment of sheet zinc that was used to cover the cupola of the old Victorian market hall when it was built in the late 1860s. The hat was removed when metal was being collected for the war effort. George Whitfield opened his ladies' wear shop in the 1920s, taking over the premises of A. and E. Edwards who ran their ladies' fancy repository from there. (*Author's Collection*)

Castle Street, *c*. 1958. The Raven Hotel was one of Shrewsbury's principal inns for well over two centuries and its importance is shown in the fact that during the eighteenth and early nineteenth centuries Castle Street was known as Raven Street. In April 1943 the hotel was commandeered and used by the American Red Cross as a Leave Club for their troops stationed here. The Americans left in August 1945 and for months rumours spread round the town about the hotel's fate. One idea was that it could be used to house young homeless couples. However, the hotel was refurbished towards the end of 1946 and reopened as a hotel on 22 February 1947. Throughout the 1950s many of the stars, such as Laurel and Hardy, Winifred Atwell, Frankie Vaughan and Lonnie Donegan, stayed at the hotel for the week while performing at the Granada Theatre. (*Abbeycolor*)

Castle Street, 1960. W.H. Smith opened this shop in Castle Street in 1906, and enlarged into the shop next door when it became vacant in 1938. The business moved to Pride Hill at the end of the 1980s into a shop vacated by Menzies. It's interesting to note that in 1866 W.H. Smith had opened a stall on Shrewsbury station, giving passengers the chance to buy books and newspapers before boarding their trains. The stall closed in about 1964. (*Abbeycolor*)

Castle Street, *c.* 1955. The impressive statue of Charles Darwin is situated in front of the school he attended as a boy. It was presented to the town by the Shropshire Horticultural Society and unveiled on 10 August 1897. The bronze statue was modelled by H. Montford and stands on a massive pedestal of polished granite. In 1997 Rosalind McGovern, Australia's Assistant High Commissioner, unveiled the refurbished statue exactly a hundred years to the day after it was first presented. The facelift, costing in the region of £8,000, was again made possible through the great generosity of the Horticultural Society. Shrewsbury School moved from this cramped site to the more open spaces of Kingsland in 1882. The timber-framed building across the road could well be the first piece of conservation in the town. The house is known as Castle Gates House and it once stood on Dogpole on the site of the Guildhall. But when Francis, Lord Newport wanted to build his new town house on that site in 1696, two years after he had been created Earl of Bradford, he had this one moved. The house was greatly restored in about 1912, when the bay windows were added. (*Author's Collection*)

Castle Gates, *c.* 1955. Shrewsbury School was founded in 1552, but the main building was not erected until 1830. Over the main entrance are the arms of King Charles I and the figures on either side represent Philamethon and Polymathan. They are in Jacobean dress and represent the student and the graduate. The plaque between them is written in Greek and reads 'If you love learning, you will learn'. The castle was founded in 1067 and was enlarged and restored between 1280 and 1300, during the reign of Edward I. Thomas Telford turned it into a dwelling for Sir William Poultney and in 1926 the main hall was transformed into a Council Chamber for the Borough Council. In the 1980s Geoffrey Archer Parfitt was responsible for bringing together and displaying the county's military history in the Castle, an achievement that won the British Tourist Authority of Merit in 1985. The steps lead to the Dana, a walk leading round the Castle from Castle Gates to the prison in Castlefields. It was named after the Revd Edward Dana, Vicar of Wroxeter and a trustee for the Shrewsbury Street Acts in 1794. (*J. Savage*)

Windsor Place, 1960. The street takes its name from Windsor House on the corner of St Mary's Place and the family that lived there. Before this it seems to have been part of St Mary's Place. The building is the rear of Wildings and was the entrance to their printing works. The firm was started by Longworth Wilding in 1875 and soon became a flourishing business. As well as the usual printing Mr Wilding also published local books, directories, town guides and postcards of the county, which are now much sought after by collectors. On the ground floor were the printing presses, on the first floor the compositors and on the top floor the bookbinders, which meant that all the finished printing had to be carried up two flights of stairs to be bound! Below the building in a warren of cellars were the paper store and the type store, where all the lead type used on a regular basis was kept on trays on large units. (*Abbeycolor*)

Castle Street, 1953. Miss Shropshire, 26-year-old Kathleen Bright from Dorrington, and her entourage add a touch of glamour to the carnival procession. She was a popular choice and was crowned in the Quarry by the Mayoress Mrs J.M. McNamara. This carnival attracted 42 decorated vehicles and over 200 walking competitors. On Mr Leach's float from Belle Vue were Dan Dare, Digby, and the rest of the *Eagle* comic's characters, while on the Frankwell Float were Queen Salote of Tonga and her Royal Court. The people of Frankwell always strongly supported the town carnival and it was the 'Little Boro' that revived the event after the war. (*J. Savage*)

Castle Street, 1953. Music and dancing was the order of the day at Shrewsbury Carnival. This was one of around a dozen jazz bands that marched through the streets of the town in the carnival procession. Frankwell Jazz Band was present: they had revived their Snow White routine that had made them Midland County Champions in 1937. There was also no lack of music as the RAF Band from Cosford, the St John's Ambulance Band, The Salopia Division Band, the Oswestry Excelsior Silver Prize Band, the Waters Upton Band and the Corps Band of REME Ellesmere were dispersed throughout the parade. (*J. Savage*)

3

The Heart of Shrewsbury

Dogpole, 1960. It has been suggested that the name is derived from 'ducken', to stoop, and 'poll', a summit, referring to a low gate that once gave access through the town wall, which crossed the lower end of the street. The correct name for the Guildhall is Newport House, as it was built by Francis, Lord Newport in 1696, two years after he had been created Earl of Bradford. This London-style town house was entirely new to Shrewsbury and set a trend that was to be copied by other wealthy Shropshire families. The Olde House is a timber-framed mansion with an attractive cobbled forecourt that dates from the early sixteenth century. At the rear of the building, overlooking the river, is a Georgian frontage. Next door is Oak House, which once housed the Shrewsbury Club, an establishment frequented by the professional and businessmen of the town. (*Abbeycolor*)

St Mary's Street and St Mary's Place, *c. 1955*. The magnificent Crown Hotel was a mock-Tudor building erected at the start of the twentieth century by the Church Stretton Hotel Company. The old Crown Hotel, which was demolished to make way for this building, was opened in an old Georgian town house in about 1780. The hotel was closed in 1940 and for the duration of the war was used as an officers' club. It was sold in October 1959 and demolished three years later to make way for the concrete and glass office block seen below. The Yorkshire House (far right) has been an inn since the early part of the nineteenth century. During the late 1950s and early '60s the landlord was Gerald Cuff, who fronted the popular '*Popeye Show*' on television as the Bosun. (*Author's Collection*)

St Mary's Street, *c.* 1964. This, photograph was taken from a similar angle to the one above and shows how the demolition of one building and its replacement can spoil the whole aspect of a small street. Crown House is a typical 1960s building of concrete and glass, which overpowers the other buildings on the street and is totally out of place next door to St Mary's church. (*Abbeycolor*)

St Mary's Street, 1960. John Carline, a local stonemason, erected the new Draper's Almshouses in 1825 on land that had been known as the Rookery. An unusual feature of the building was that the people who lived to the left of the entrance were in the parish of St Alkmund, while the people to the right were in the parish of St Mary. The head post office next door was opened in 1877 and was built on the site of the old Butter Market. At the far end is the impressive frontage of Morris's main store. It was opened in 1927; the architect based his design on Blickling Hall in Norfolk. (*Abbeycolor*)

The junction of Pride Hill and St Mary's Street, *c.* 1965. The open space is where the old Draper's Almshouses stood. They were demolished in May 1964 and the residents moved into the new sheltered accommodation off Greyfriars Road. The new post office was opened in June 1964 by Councillor Frank Ellis, the Mayor of Shrewsbury. He was also the first customer, purchasing a 5s book of stamps. The cost of the new building was around £142,000. The Midland Electricity Board opened a new showroom on the corner and was there for a number of years, until Burger King opened their new restaurant on the site. (*Abbeycolor*)

St Mary's Street, 1960. W.W. Humphreys was established in 1815 and sold fine wines and spirits. The building was erected on the courtyard of Jones's Mansion, which it completely obscures. Next door is the long frontage of the Draper's Almshouses, which was restored in 1897. They contained seventeen dwellings, each with two small rooms. There was no running water or toilet facilities within the cottages. The post office on the corner cost around £7,300 plus £1,000 for fittings. It was built out of red brick, with Grinshill stone dressing and a roof covered in green Bangor slate. (*Abbeycolor*)

St Mary's Place, 1960. This section of road was once known as St Mary's Church Yard. The Yorkshire House is timber-framed but has had a brick cladding placed around it to modernise it, a common practice in the eighteenth century. The timber-framed house next door is known as the Verger's House or St Mary's Cottages and dates from the seventeenth century. Running to the right of the cottages is St Mary's Shut, which brings pedestrians out on to Castle Street next to Sidoli's café. In about 1805 it was known as Little Shut. The petrol pumps are a relic of the old Crown garage and car park. In the 1930s you could park there all day for just 1s. The wooden building is the temporary head post office, used while the new one was being built in St Mary's Street between November 1959 and June 1964. At the bottom of the street is the unusual rounded wall of Windsor House. The building was erected in the eighteenth century and possesses an elegant classical doorway on its Windsor Place frontage. (*Abbeycolor*)

St Mary's Place, 1960. This street once had a turnstile at its entrance near the Draper's Hall, which was replaced in 1836 by some iron gates. The street has also been known as the Turnstile or just the Close. The Royal Salop Infirmary was erected in 1830. It was founded in 1747 in a Georgian town house on that site and was reputed to be only the fifth in the country at that time. The architect was Edward Haycock, and it was one of the first large buildings in England to be fitted with hot water central heating. The hospital was closed in 1977, and the ground floor and basement have been converted into exclusive shop units while the upper floors have been transformed into luxury apartments. (*Abbeycolor*)

Doctors and surgeons at the Royal Salop Infirmary, 1963. Back row, left to right: Dr A.T.M. Myers, Mr P. Britten, Dr C.R.H. Jenkins, Dr R. Turner, Dr M.C.J. McCloy, Dr M.D. Enoch, Mr R.S. Cowie. Third row: Dr Littlejohn, Dr A.C. Jones, Dr P.E. Percival, Dr J.C. Macaulay, Dr P. McQuaide, Dr E.G. Rees, Dr F. McKane, Mr Livesey. Second row: Dr J.J. Polland, Mr S. Burke, Dr J.M. Bryson, Dr M. Symons, Mr C. Taylor, Mr H.G. Wolskel, Mr E.N. Owen, Dr E. Richardson. Front row: Mr A. Glandon Williams, Dr Doreen Davies, Dr H. Foy, Mr D. Lincoln Lewis, Dr C. Lawson Stote, Mr J.A. Baty, Dr Sophie Lucus, Dr W.D. Wallace, Mr A. Russell Johnson. The dog's name was Seal. (*Author's Collection*)

The view from the rear of the Royal Salop Infirmary, 1959. During the night of 5 February a huge landslide occurred at the rear of the hospital. Tons of earth fell from the embankment, tearing a chasm over 30 ft wide and exposing the foundations of the building. Expert engineers were called in to save the building, while several patients were evacuated and the maternity unit transferred to Copthorne Hospital. It took several months and tons of concrete and earth to make the building safe again. The incident could have been the final nail in the coffin for the old hospital, as it was announced in January 1960 that plans were being drawn up to replace the RSI with a new general hospital on another site. (*Abbeycolor*)

St Mary's Street to Dogpole, 1960. In the 1950s Pat-a-Cake's was listed as tearooms and home bakery, but by the 1960s it was a high-class confectioner's with a licensed restaurant. In 1921 Winchester House was a boarding house run by James Ward, but by 1929 it was listed as the Winchester House Private Hotel. The hotel was closed shortly after this photograph was taken and the ground floor was transformed into a shop for European Office Supplies Ltd, who sold office equipment. (*Abbeycolor*)

Butcher Row, 1960. The street was once called the Flesh Shambles, shambles being the name given to stalls in a town set up for the use of butchers and fishmongers. The street was known later as Double Butcher Row to distinguish it from Single Butcher Row on Pride Hill. During the eighteenth and early nineteenth centuries butchers' stalls extended down the left-hand side of Pride Hill from the area of Burger King, up Butcher Row and down Fish Street to St Julian's Church. In 1828 sixteen butchers' shops are listed in Pride Hill, fifteen in Butcher Row and nine in Fish Street. As there was no abattoir in the town at this time, most of the animals were slaughtered on site. (*Abbeycolor*)

Butcher Row, 1960. The Abbot Studios occupies part of the ancient Abbot's House, built in about 1500, from where the business takes its name; it was a professional photographer. Before that F.R. Hockney, an antiques dealer, occupied the shop. An advert for the travel agent next door read 'Whether you travel near or far, for business or for pleasure, always consult Severn Travel Bureau, for efficient and personal service'. Beyond there is the rear of Maddox Store. Note one of the old No Waiting signs that were introduced in the late 1950s. (*Author's Collection*)

St Alkmund's Place, *c.* 1955. The Bear Steps complex stands at the very heart of medieval Shrewsbury. It contains two bays of a three-bay hall dating from the fourteenth century and an arcade of shops, built at a later date. The third bay of the hall was lost in the early 1950s when it was demolished along with other buildings to make a wider access into St Alkmund's Square; the public toilets now occupy the site of the third bay. The whole complex was under threat of demolition at one time, but thankfully they were saved by the newly formed Shrewsbury Civic Society in about 1968 (note the sign), and the society's offices are now located in part of the building. The name of the complex comes from the Bear Inn that occupied the building opposite the steps on the corner of Fish Street and Grope Lane. The inn was there from around 1780 until 1910 and was occasionally referred to as the Old Bear or the White Bear. (*J. Savage*)

Fish Street, *c.* 1955. The street was once known as Chepynstrete, an old word for Market Street, the market at that time being based in St Alkmund's Square. The church of St Alkmund (back), with the exception of the tower and spire, was rebuilt by Tilley and Carline between 1794 and 1795. The pinnacles at the base of the spire were added in 1897 and are a memorial to the Revd John Wightman, vicar of St Alkmund's in the second half of the nineteenth century. His widow Julia, who was a great temperance fighter, presented them. The steps lead to St Julian's Church, another of the town's medieval churches rebuilt in the eighteenth century. At the top of the steps near the main doorway is the grave of Samuel Hayward, the driver of the Shrewsbury to London mail coach, the *Wonder*. After sixteen years of driving the coach he became the landlord of the Raven and Bell. Always a popular and friendly man, he asked to be buried near the church door so people walking into the building would remember him. Phillips Stores acquired this shop (left) in the 1920s from Bagnall & Brown. The shop was known as the Golden Canister Store from a large trade sign hanging outside. (*Author's Collection*)

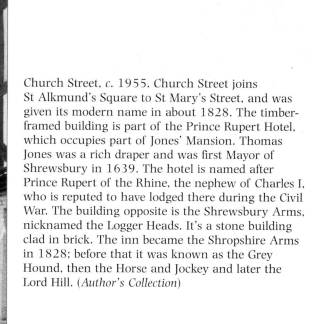

Church Street, *c.* 1955. Church Street joins St Alkmund's Square to St Mary's Street, and was given its modern name in about 1828. The timber-framed building is part of the Prince Rupert Hotel, which occupies part of Jones' Mansion. Thomas Jones was a rich draper and was first Mayor of Shrewsbury in 1639. The hotel is named after Prince Rupert of the Rhine, the nephew of Charles I, who is reputed to have lodged there during the Civil War. The building opposite is the Shrewsbury Arms, nicknamed the Logger Heads. It's a stone building clad in brick. The inn became the Shropshire Arms in 1828; before that it was known as the Grey Hound, then the Horse and Jockey and later the Lord Hill. (*Author's Collection*)

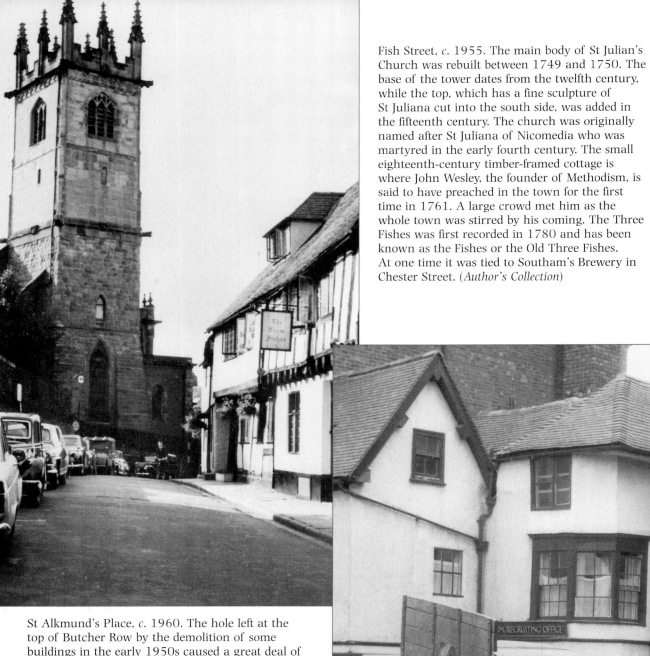

Fish Street, *c.* 1955. The main body of St Julian's Church was rebuilt between 1749 and 1750. The base of the tower dates from the twelfth century, while the top, which has a fine sculpture of St Juliana cut into the south side, was added in the fifteenth century. The church was originally named after St Juliana of Nicomedia who was martyred in the early fourth century. The small eighteenth-century timber-framed cottage is where John Wesley, the founder of Methodism, is said to have preached in the town for the first time in 1761. A large crowd met him as the whole town was stirred by his coming. The Three Fishes was first recorded in 1780 and has been known as the Fishes or the Old Three Fishes. At one time it was tied to Southam's Brewery in Chester Street. (*Author's Collection*)

St Alkmund's Place, *c.* 1960. The hole left at the top of Butcher Row by the demolition of some buildings in the early 1950s caused a great deal of controversy. Alderman Sam Powell labelled it the Black Hole of Calcutta in February 1960, more than five years after it had first appeared. One councillor was so appalled by the lack of progress that he commented: 'I am told this hole has been taken over by the Ministry of Works because it's been there so long it has become an ancient monument.' The public toilets built by Boswells now occupy the site. The buildings opposite were owned by Roy Fletcher, who let the top room above the bay window to the Scouts as their county office, a religious group had a meeting hall there and there was also a work-recruiting agency on the ground floor. Victor Hendel redeveloped the site with the extension of his hotel, the Prince Rupert. (*Author's Collection*)

4

Mardol

The Welsh Bridge to Mardol Quay, *c.* 1955. This section of road leading from the Quarry to the Welsh Bridge is now known as Victoria Quay and is where the *River King*, the town's latest pleasure cruiser, is moored. The new Welsh Bridge was erected several yards downstream from the old one. It was built by Shrewsbury builders Tilley and Carline at a cost of £8,000. The gauge on the left was fitted to the riverbed in the 1950s so that the water board could take a more accurate reading of the height of the river over a twenty-four hour period. It proved a great attraction during the floods of the 1960s. Note the old halt sign at the junction and the side of Gethin's Garage over the road. (*J. Savage*)

Mardol to Mardol Quay, *c.* 1960. Frank Gethin opened this garage in 1921 after returning home from India, and was the sole proprietor of the business until his death in 1959, when the land was sold to the borough for road widening and the development of a riverside park. David Hing opened the Hung Hing Restaurant at the end of the 1950s. It was the town's first Chinese restaurant and in the early days they served a businessman's lunch, consisting of a main course, sweet and tea or coffee for just *2s 3d.* That building had been a restaurant since the nineteenth century, first as Hilliers and then as the Galleon Restaurant. The King's Head is housed in one of the most attractive of Shrewsbury's half-timbered buildings. It was listed as the Last Inn from 1780 until around 1820 when its present name was transferred from an inn further up Mardol. The king it represents is Henry VII, who, as Henry Tudor, marched through Shrewsbury to fight the battle at Market Bosworth, which put him on the English throne. (*Author's Collection*)

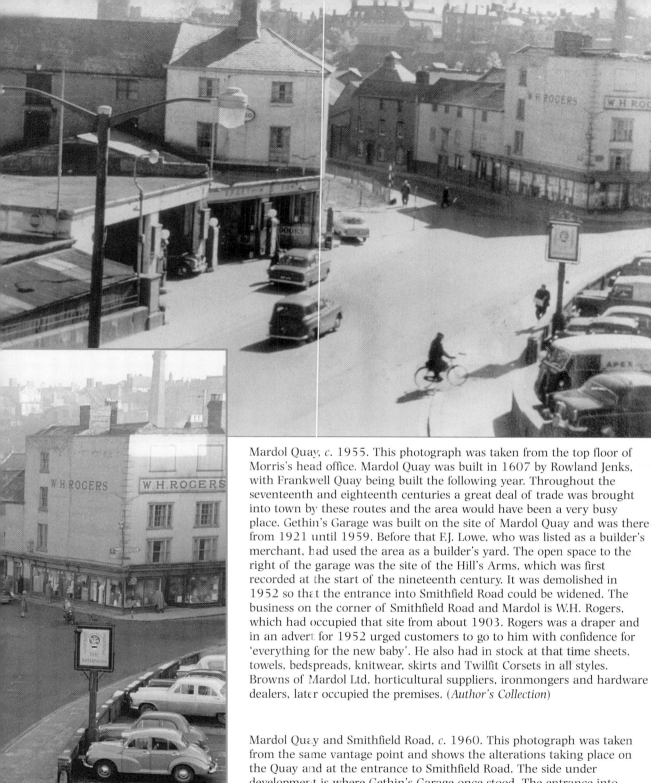

Mardol Quay, *c.* 1955. This photograph was taken from the top floor of Morris's head office. Mardol Quay was built in 1607 by Rowland Jenks, with Frankwell Quay being built the following year. Throughout the seventeenth and eighteenth centuries a great deal of trade was brought into town by these routes and the area would have been a very busy place. Gethin's Garage was built on the site of Mardol Quay and was there from 1921 until 1959. Before that F.J. Lowe, who was listed as a builder's merchant, had used the area as a builder's yard. The open space to the right of the garage was the site of the Hill's Arms, which was first recorded at the start of the nineteenth century. It was demolished in 1952 so that the entrance into Smithfield Road could be widened. The business on the corner of Smithfield Road and Mardol is W.H. Rogers, which had occupied that site from about 1903. Rogers was a draper and in an advert for 1952 urged customers to go to him with confidence for 'everything for the new baby'. He also had in stock at that time sheets, towels, bedspreads, knitwear, skirts and Twilfit Corsets in all styles. Browns of Mardol Ltd, horticultural suppliers, ironmongers and hardware dealers, later occupied the premises. (*Author's Collection*)

Mardol Quay and Smithfield Road, *c.* 1960. This photograph was taken from the same vantage point and shows the alterations taking place on the Quay and at the entrance to Smithfield Road. The side under development is where Gethin's Garage once stood. The entrance into Smithfield Road had been widened in 1952, after the demolition of the Hill's Arms, but with the increase in road traffic it was still too narrow. The curbstones of the widened road can be seen curving around to Smithfield Road on the left. The remaining land was used as a little riverside park. Note the big wheel just below the castle; it belonged to Deek's fun fair, which used to stay on the cattle market site before it was redeveloped. (*Author's Collection*)

Mardol Quay, *c.* 1960. Ideas to beautify the river at the bottom of Mardol were looked at by the Council as early as June 1957 and by February 1959 a £36,500 improvement plan had been drawn up. In the background is the Welsh Bridge and to the left of the bridge is Hall's office and saleroom. The building had once been Mr Bromley's seed warehouse and had been built on the site of an old inn called the Squirrel. To the right of the bridge is Frankwell Forge, while just above is St George's church, built as a chapel of ease in Mountfields in 1832. (*Abbeycolor*)

Mardol Quay, 1960. This is a view taken from the Welsh Bridge of the site once occupied by Gethin's Garage. As well as the garage, Swain's warehouse was removed and a number of slum properties demolished under a clearance order from the Public Health Committee. The lower part of the stonewall would have been part of the quay; note the flight of steps and the large culvert, which empties the stream that rises in the Square into the Severn. The building on the right is the Britannia Hotel, now the Shropshire Arms. (*Abbeycolor*)

Mardol, 1960. Ye Olde Baccy Shoppe had been a tobacconist and newsagent's shop since the nineteenth century, when a saddler occupied half the premises. Since this photograph was taken the plaster has been removed and instead of the ornate features we see drawn on the plaster a plainer timber frame was exposed, leading some people to suppose it had not been built as a dwelling, but for some other unknown purpose. The timbers are well preserved and there are some nice carpenter's marks cut into them. Two generations of the Holyoake family ran the shop: they were also fishing tackle specialists, selling all the leading makes of rod and tackle including Hardy, Alcock and Milward. (*Abbeycolor*)

Mardol, 1960. Lord and Lady Berwick opened the Empire cinema on 25 November 1922. It became the first picture house in the county to introduce the 'Talkies' with the film *Movietone Follies*. The wide-screen Cinemascope was installed in April 1955 and the film, *How To Marry A Millionaire*, starring Marilyn Monroe and Betty Grable, was the first film to be shown in that medium. With the coming of the multi-screen cinema the days of the Empire were numbered and it finally closed in 1998, with the site being turned into a pizza parlour and a Yates Wine Lodge. The building to the left of the cinema belonged to F.H. Burgess Ltd, which was an ironmonger, hardware dealer and agricultural engineer. The yard was big enough to store large farming implements, and with a rear entrance on to Roushill they were ideally situated to attract farmers from the Smithfield cattle market. Before the ironmonger moved in, the building was a hotel known as the Queens. Meesons confectionery shop was once known as the Salop Pure Sweet Shop, and was run for many years by Mr and Mrs Lockley. (*Abbeycolor*)

Mardol and Roushill, 1960. This was the narrow entrance into Roushill from Mardol before the road system was redeveloped in the Raven Meadow's area towards the end of the 1960s. Richard Bromley was born at Yockleton, where he worked on the family farm and managed the local mill. After buying the mill he opened up a shop to sell grain at 18 Mardol before moving to these premises. He was elected on to the council in 1901, representing the Welsh Ward. He was Mayor of Shrewsbury in 1925 and an Alderman from 1917 until his death in 1936. Boots had their chemist shop on the other corner for a short time in the 1960s. The house was built in the late sixteenth century and now houses a small restaurant. It has a strange little dragon climbing up the outside wall. (*Abbeycolor*)

Mardol, 1960. William Gowan Cross became apprenticed to a chemist at 70 Mardol, a business he bought in 1847, and his son, also named William Gowan, carried on the business. Both men were Mayors of Shrewsbury, the father in 1875–6 and again in 1879, and the son in 1893–4. In October 1958 Cross Bros, Wholesale Photographic Finishers, W.G. Cross & Son, Chemist, Wine Merchants & Photographic Dealer, and Bernard Cross Photographers, became W.G. Cross & Sons Ltd. The company was able to provide practically every photographic service available. They had a miniature theatre seating twelve, for demonstrating cine film and equipment, and had Shrewsbury's only 8mm film library; they also hired out 16mm sound projectors and made movie films of big family occasions. Their developing and printing department turned out thousands of prints each day and there was a photographic studio for portrait, wedding and commercial photography. The business remained in the family until Abbeycolor took them over. (*Abbeycolor*)

Beddard's shop, Mardol, *c.* 1960. Helen Moden holds one of Charlie Beddard's famous pork pies, made from his own recipe. He came to the town from the West Midlands in 1913, opening a shop on Wyle Cop, before transferring to Mardol in 1917. As well as pork pies his home-cured bacon and ham, pig's trotters and pork sausages were much sought after, and a particular delicacy for many local families on a Friday lunchtime was a portion of chitterlings, the small intestines of pigs, served steaming hot and wrapped up in old newspaper. The business was sold to Gaskell Brothers of Warrington in 1965. (*Author's Collection*)

Mardol, 8 August 1951. Briggs shoe shop is part of a national chain and has been trading in Mardol since the early part of the twentieth century. The staff are shown here. Standing, left to right: Mr King (manager), Mr Denfy. Seated: Mrs Pykes, Mrs Plumb, Miss Edwards and Miss Williams. Two other staff were absent: Miss Edgly was away sick while Miss Blackmore was on holiday. (*Author's Collection*)

Mardol Head and Shoplatch, 1960. Before 1825 Mardol Head was known as Le Stalls and was at one time the area where the booksellers had their shops. There was an ancient inn called the Bear on the left-hand side, next to Gullet Passage. It was mentioned in a deed as early as November 1610. On the right is Jackson, the tailor, which is next door to W.J. Jones, the dispensing and photographic chemist. He had premises on Wyle Cop and at 16 Pride Hill, where he also had an optician's. The old Victorian Market Hall takes up the whole of the right-hand side of Shoplatch. The large white building on the left is the George Hotel, while the street beyond Shoplatch is St John's Hill. (*Abbeycolor*)

The junction of High Street and Mardol Head, *c.* 1962. Erected at the beginning of the twentieth century, the Royal Insurance's new offices stand well alongside the older Ireland's Mansion. The site was once occupied by their own fire station on the Mardol Head side and a draper's shop, belonging to a Mr Landon, on the corner. The shops to the right of the office were demolished in 1971. The lady on the right was a flower seller and is standing outside the new tailor's shop belonging to John Collier. It was opened in 1962 and advertised as 'the shop with a fascinating secret', as parts of the ancient Benet's Hall were incorporated into the new building. (*Abbeycolor*)

5

Around the Market Hall

Barker Street, *c.* 1964. The new Market Hall and the modern buildings on Claremont Street do not blend in well with the ancient timbers of Rowley's House in the foreground. The Market Hall was opened for business in November 1964, but the tower, which was behind schedule, was not completed until March the following year. The foundations of the tower were dug out by hand and the completed structure was built out of 50,000 bricks. The bare brick building between Rowley's House and the Market is the Baptist church in Claremont Street. It was erected between 1878 and 1879 and has a very ornate frontage, complete with two pairs of Corinthian pilasters. (*Abbeycolor*)

The Victorian Market Hall, Mardol Head, *c. 1960*. This was the main entrance to the arcade, which ran through to the Butchers' Market where forty-six stalls and four shops were provided for the town and county butchers. The arcade contained a number of shops, a refreshment room run by Frank Machin and a dining room run by Mrs Mary Bennett. Over the entrance is the date the Market opened and above that, beautifully carved in Grinshill stone, is a copy of the town coat of arms, the Logger Heads. The man by the front steps is selling the Sunday newspapers. (*Abbeycolor*)

The Victorian Market Hall, Claremont Street, *c.* 1960. This is a magnificent view of the Market Hall looking up Claremont Street towards Timpson's shoe shop. There were eight entrances into the market of which six were in daily use. Beneath the building were a number of vaults and warehouses, which could be accessed from this side of the building by a cartway that was covered by a glass roof so that goods could be loaded and unloaded in bad weather. The round windows under the tower are part of the Corn Exchange, later taken over as a public billiard hall. Barkworths, on the right, were fishmongers, who also had another shop in Mardol. (*Abbeycolor*)

The Victorian Market Hall, Claremont Street and Belstone, *c.* 1960. The superintendent's offices and stores were located at the Belstone end of the market, as was the wholesale market, which was raised about a foot above the main market hall; there were toilet facilities for ladies and gentlemen at this end of the building. This corner of the building was once occupied by the Borough Fire Brigade, which kept its fire appliance there from 1918 until 1938 when they moved to their new station on Cross Hill. One of the pinnacles above the clock and part of the metal clock face still survive, preserved in the rockery of a garden just outside Shrewsbury. (*Abbeycolor*)

The Victorian Market Hall, Belstone and Shoplatch, *c.* 1960. The tower rose to a height of 151 ft and was topped by an ornamental iron vane, which was considered 'exceedingly handsome' at the time. It was a square tower and had a clock dial on each side that was illuminated green at night. Joyce of Whitchurch made the clock while the bell was cast by the founders Mears & Stainbane of London. Both the clock and bell were paid for by public subscription. The doors and windows of the building were all circular headed and the majority of the doors were sliding instead of hinged. (*Abbeycolor*)

The interior of the Victorian Market Hall, *c.* 1960. The market was open each day but the most important were held on Wednesdays and Saturdays. The hall was described as spacious, well ventilated and lit throughout with electricity. There were seventeen fruit, flower, confectionery and fish stalls set around the perimeter of the hall, with 117 benches and 57 double-sided seats in the centre for the use of the farmers' wives and the market gardeners who brought their produce on the main market days. The hall was also used as a corn exchange on a Saturday, for wool and cheese sales at different times of the year and as a Christmas poultry market about a fortnight before Christmas. (*Author's Collection*)

The new Market Hall, *c.* 1964. This view was taken from the tower of St Chad's church. The market tenants moved out of the Belstone end of the old market hall and into the new Mardol end in June 1963. Apart from the new Market Hall this photograph show the scale of redevelopment that was going on in the town at this time. To the left of St Mary's church are the new Barclay's Bank, Crown House and post office. In front of the church is the open space left after the demolition of the almshouses. There is another open space on the corner of Shoplatch and Market Street, created by the demolition of the George Hotel, and on the left of the market are some new buildings in Claremont Street. The building in the foreground is the rear of the Morris Hall. (*Abbeycolor*)

Aerial view of the new Market Hall, *c.* 1970. The two aerial views on this page were taken by Roy Pilsbury and show the visual impact the new Market Hall had on the landscape of the town. When the plans for the new market were drawn up in 1957 they included a large restaurant and roof garden, but these never materialised. In the foreground are Rowley's House and Mansion and the bus station. Mardol is the street on the left, while Barker Street and Belstone are on the right. Tesco's new store can be seen just above the market on the site of the George Hotel, and at the top, just to the right of centre, is the old fire station that was demolished in 1976. (*R. Pitsburg*)

Aerial view of the new Market Hall, *c.* 1970. The shape of the Mardol end of the market hall has been likened to a coffin while the tower at the Belstone end has featured as a view in a competition for the worst postcard ever sold. The rooflines of the Square in the foreground and those of Mardol to the right and Hill's Lane, top centre, compare well with the market, the new buildings in Claremont Street and the black oblong shape of the Trustees Saving Bank on the corner of Swan Hill and Market Street. (*R. Pitsburg*)

Shoplatch, 1964. The name of this street in 1300 was Scheteplache, derived from the place or residence of the Schutte family. In the eighteenth century the area from Market Street to the junction of Belstone and St John's Hill was known as Carrier's End, perhaps because of the carriers' carts that would have stopped in the vicinity of the George Hotel. For a short time after the building of the Victorian Market Hall part of the street became known as Newmarket Place. During the autumn of 1964 the road was widened to 30 ft. Diversions were needed for a number of weeks, but the authorities hoped to have the work completed by November and before the Christmas rush. In the last few years the width has been reduced by half as part of the town's traffic calming measures. (*Author's Collection*)

St John's Hill, *c.* 1955. This smart young man and his dog walk boldly towards the photographer, on their way home after a shopping trip into town. In 1647 the fish stalls were taken away from the wall below St Julian's church and placed in this area at the bottom of the hill for a short time, before first moving to the Green Market in the Square and then back to Fish Street in 1763. The shop with the cigarette vending machine is a newsagent and tobacconist owned by John Holyoake, the owner of Ye Olde Baccy Shoppe in Mardol. (*Author's Collection*)

St John's Hill, *c.* 1955. Until the sixteenth century this street was considered an extension of Shoplatch. It became known as St John's Hill because the hospital of St John in Frankwell once owned a great deal of property in the area. During the eighteenth century the street was often referred to as Swine Market Hill as the pig market had been held there for many years. The large Georgian house at the top is Hardwick House, built by the Revd Dr Robert Phillips, who was headmaster of Shrewsbury School from 1727 until 1735. In the garden is a beautiful eighteenth-century summerhouse with a flight of steps on either side of the doorway. The children are walking past the shop belonging to Livesey the printers. A Mr Wardle founded the business on Pride Hill in 1843. He moved to these premises, which were connected to a large printing works on Cross Hill, in about 1880. Joseph Livesey, a native of Preston, bought the firm in about 1890. The firm still trades in the town but has moved to a new modern factory on Longdon Road. (*Author's Collection*)

The Exchange and Mart, St John's Hill, 1960. This shop was also known as Fortunate Finds and was run by Howard Newman in the 1950s and '60s. It was a Mecca for all budding philatelists and cigarette card collectors as he had stock books bulging with postage stamps from all over the world, and you could purchase a pack of ten assorted cigarette cards for 3d up to a full set of fifty for as little as 2s 6d. On a Saturday morning after the matinee at the Empire the shop would be full of children looking at the stuffed alligator in the entrance and the variety of African spears and shields in the main shop. Mr Newman also sold a variety of second-hand sports equipment and guaranteed all year round repairs for tennis rackets. (Abbeycolor)

Murivance to St Chad's Terrace, c. 1955. The name Murivance originates from two French words, 'mur avant', meaning before or within the walls, thought to refer to a large open space used by soldiers to parade. It was known as St John's Row or Wall Lane, before the town wall was removed. Before the building of the church, St Chad's Terrace was known as Quarry Alley, and was a lane that ran outside the town wall between St John's Hill and Claremont Hill. The first stone of St Chad's church was laid on St Chad's Day, 2 March 1790, and the new church was consecrated on 19 August 1792. Its unusual design was the work of George Stewart, the architect of Attingham Hall. Quarry Place, on the left, was once known as Duck Lane. (Abbeycolor)

Claremont Hill, 1960. The name of the hill can be traced back to the thirteenth century and originates from the Norman French words 'clare', a residence, and 'mont', a hill. The street contains a mixture of architecture from Tudor to Georgian, while up alleyways like Draper's Court are some attractive timber-framed cottages. (*Abbeycolor*)

Claremont Street, 1960. Apart from Evans's newspaper shop, now the Star Shop, all the buildings on the right, as far as the railings, were demolished in the early 1960s. Parkhurst & Walker sold groceries and cooked meat, while Mr Embrey next door was a butcher. The New Market Vaults was renamed in 1868 during the building of the Market Hall. Before this it was known as the Golden Hart. It was tied to Trouncer's Brewery and was demolished in 1963. (*Abbeycolor*)

Claremont Hill to Barker Street, 1960. The hairdresser's belonged to Mr Mumford. Since this photograph the business has moved next door into the craft shop. The barber's shop is now Rhodes' chemist shop and the National Milk Bar on the corner is now Kentucky Fried Chicken. The large building across the road is the side of the Claremont Baptist church. It was rebuilt between 1877 and 1878 on the site they had used since 1780. The people are queuing for their S1 or S21 bus to Monkmoor. (*Abbeycolor*)

Belstone, Barker Street and Claremont Hill, 1960. The Little Fruit Market was owned by S.J. Richards, who opened the business in about 1938. The building was occupied by Sidoli's as a café from the mid-1960s. They also had a shop next door and one of their ice-cream vans can be seen outside the greengrocer's. Mr D. Mumford ran the gents' hairdressers at the bottom of Claremont Hill for many years; it is now a chemist's shop. The National Milk Bar had only recently opened and was one of three in the town during the 1960s. They took the premises over from Mr Shaw, a local butcher. (*Abbeycolor*)

Belstone, 1960. These buildings were erected in the 1930s when Belstone and Barker Street were widened as part of an inner ring road and car-parking scheme. Many old properties were demolished here, including a small Elizabethan mansion known as Bellstone House. By the 1930s much of the mansion had been hidden by a modern frontage, which housed the National Provincial Bank. The new buildings were built in a neo-Tudor style and named Old Bank Buildings. Through the archway are the Morris Hall and an ancient boulder of glacial origin, known as the 'Bell Stone', which gives the street its name. (*Abbeycolor*)

Barker Street, 1960. At one time the bus station was in the Square, but after 1945, when the need for public transport grew, a larger station was required. For a while a temporary station was set up on the site now occupied by the multi-storey car park in Bridge Street. In January 1952 this site was opened and within the month it was declared a great success. The one-way system for buses in and out of the station and the permanent stands made it more convenient for passengers. A canteen was set up for the staff in a building in Hill's Lane that had once been the Old Gullet Inn, and in 1960 a purpose-built canteen and restroom had been opened for them behind the bus on the extreme left. The bus station moved to Raven Meadow in 1992. (*Abbeycolor*)

Rowley's House, Barker Street, *c.* 1960. Before the demolition of the buildings in the Bridge Street, Hill's Lane and Barker Street area, few people knew of the existence of Rowley's House as it was completely hidden by buildings on all sides. As the other buildings were pulled down it became obvious to Arthur Ward, the Borough Surveyor, that Rowley's House was worth preserving. A rescue plan was drawn up to save the building and a great deal of material from the demolished houses was used in its restoration. The only concessions Ward made was that a passageway was put through the middle of the building to link the two car parks on either side, and several feet were taken off the ground-floor area facing Barker Street to make a pavement. The floor above was supported on massive timbers, like the House on Crutches in Bishop's Castle. William Rowley, a draper and brewer who was born in Worfield near Bridgnorth, built the house. It has been estimated that at least a hundred fully grown oak trees were used in its construction. (*Abbeycolor*)

Barker Street and Bridge Street, *c.* 1964. This view, taken from the top of the New Market clocktower, is dominated by the multi-storey car park that was opened in time for the Flower Show of August 1963. It had parking for around 430 cars and Furrow's had a small petrol station on the forecourt. To the right of the petrol pumps there was one of the town's first car washes. It was advertised as 'Quick and Easy', the driver never having to leave his seat, and costing only 7s 6d. The new buildings above and to the left of the car park are in New Street. They are known as Quarry View and were built on the site of Maddox's Buildings. Demolition is also in progress on the Frankwell Roundabout site. (*Abbeycolor*)

Barker Street, 1960. The ancient name for this area of the town was Romaldsham, named after the land belonging to the chapel, dedicated to St Romald. The buildings on the left were all rebuilt during the 1930s. The Midland Red enquiry office and cloakroom is next to the showroom of Thomasson & Holland, the electrical engineers. To the right is the shop of George Willocks & Sons, decorators, painters and heraldic designers. Next door is Eagle House, the mock-Tudor building erected for the Eagle Star Insurance Co. Ltd, which also housed Wiseman & Pook, the estate agents. (*Abbeycolor*)

Bridge Street, 1960. This street was once known as Cripple Loade or Cripple Gate and is derived from the old English words 'crypel-geat', meaning a low opening in a wall, in this case a sewer or stream running through the town wall and into the Severn. It was also called the Gulph, which means a drain or sewer. The street was given its modern name after the building of the new Welsh Bridge in 1795. There are car parks on both sides of the road. The one on the left was developed into the multi-storey car park that is due to be demolished this year, 2002. On the far right is Hill's Lane and behind the white posts Carnarvon Lane, linking Hill's Lane with Mardol. It is thought to be named after Ludovick Carnarvon who was living close by in about 1460. (*Abbeycolor*)

Barker Street, 7 August 1966. This devastating fire gutted the premises of A.D. Foulkes, a local ironmonger and building supply merchant, causing over £1 million worth of damage. At the height of the fire loud thuds could be heard as calor gas containers and tins of paint exploded in the heat. A much bigger crash was heard as stock and machinery crashed through the upper floors. Windowpanes exploded sending showers of glass down on to the road. At one point flames were seen leaping over 20 ft above the roof, and the biggest fear was that if the wind changed direction a number of other properties, including a petrol station and a gunsmith's, could be threatened. (*Author's Collection*)

Barker Street, 7 August 1966. The fire also destroyed a wool warehouse next door where wool was graded and stored for the British Wool Marketing Board. It was estimated that around 250 tons of wool worth about £128,000 were destroyed in the blaze, as well as all the grading machinery. The warehouse was almost full at the time with wool collected from all around Shropshire, Radnorshire, Worcestershire and other neighbouring counties. The manager, Mr J.K. Leigh, reported that everything had been lost and that the future of the warehouse was in the balance. (*Author's Collection*)

Barker Street, 8 August 1966. The following day thirty employees working for Foulkes were back at the site and, with smoke still rising from the burnt-out shell of their old warehouse, were erecting a wooden shed as a new depot to be back in business the next day. Within the week the hut had become a new warehouse, and office and clerical staff had been transferred across the road into a shop in Hill's Lane. Looking to the future, the manager believed that the firm would rebuild on the same site. An interesting fact is that half a century before another devastating fire had affected this site, when Cocks Tannery was burned down on 20 December 1916. Shrewsbury Sixth Form College now occupies the buildings. (*Author's Collection*)

6

From Smithfield Road to Coton Hill

Mardol Quay and Smithfield Road, *c.* 1962. This photograph was taken from the top of Morris's and shows one of the floods that affected the town during the early 1960s. The wider access into Smithfield Road can clearly be seen but the new park to the immediate left of the railings has been submerged by the Severn. The old Smithfield Cattle Market is being developed, with Telephone House being the first building to be occupied towards the end of 1962. The building has always been considered an eyesore by the people of Shrewsbury and will be demolished later this year, 2002. On the skyline, just to the right of the trees on Frankwell car park, is the gasworks in Castle Foregate, and just to the right of that is the newly built office block belonging to British Rail Western Region. (*Author's Collection*)

Smithfield Road, 1960. Plans for this road were being discussed in August 1832, with the road almost completed by June 1835. It was the very first designated road within the loop of the river at that time. The wall with the advertising boards is the boundary of the cattle market and the large roofline above it belongs to the Granada cinema. The building with Border Ales written on the side of it is the Victoria Inn. It was set up in about 1856, not long after the opening of the cattle market, to cater for the farmers that came to town on Market Day. As well as the usual bars it had accommodation for twelve travellers in five bedrooms. There were also good stabling facilities, with twenty-one stalls, seven looseboxes and accommodation for another sixteen horses in loose stabling. To the right of the inn are two established Shrewsbury firms, Medlicott Bros, radio and electrical repairs, and Shuker and Sons Ltd, agricultural suppliers. Both firms had outlets in other parts of the town. (*Abbeycolor*)

Smithfield Road, 19 August 1956. Circuses have always been a great attraction in the town. In the nineteenth century Sanger's Circus was a regular visitor to the town, pitching its big top either on the Gay Meadow or in the Quarry. Buffalo Bill's Wild West Show visited the town at the start of the twentieth century and Rosaire's Mammoth Circus was also a visitor. By the 1950s Frankwell's County Ground was the venue for all circuses and fun fairs, and regular visitors to the town at this time were Bertram Mills, Billy Smart and Chipperfield's circuses. The camels belong to Bertram Mills and have just arrived at the railway station from their last venue. On the right is the wall of the old cattle market. (*Abbeycolor*)

Raven Meadow, *c.* 1960. Although the pens have gone a flooded River Severn laps up over the deserted cattle market site. The white building in the centre is the Victoria Inn, while the trees in the background are on the other side of the river in Frankwell. The building behind the trees on the right is Atlas Foundry, which was demolished in March 2002. The building with the rounded top is the sales room belonging to auctioneers Hall, Wateridge and Owen. (*Abbeycolor*)

Raven Meadows, 1960. After the removal of the cattle market the pens and buildings were demolished and the area was used as a car park. The white building in the centre is occupied by C.R. Birch and Son and is one of the town's oldest surviving family businesses. In the 1950s they were listed as oil merchants and ironmongers. To the left of Birch's is the old Malt House and then the back entrance into Burgess's yard, now Mardol Gardens. The high roof on the extreme left is the rear of the Empire Cinema, demolished in 2001. (*Abbeycolor*)

Raven Meadows, *c.* 1962. It took around seven years for this site to be fully developed, with several plans being scrapped or drastically altered. At one stage the developers were going to include a bowling alley, a riverside restaurant and a luxury hotel, but all these were dropped. The building of Telephone House remained on schedule and it was ready for occupation in 1962. During 1993 the centre was completely redeveloped and is now part of the Pride Hill Centre: extra car parking space has been added to the multi-storey car park and the bus station has been moved here from Barker Street. As you can see, while the council and the developers argued about the site, workers and shoppers used it as a car park. (*Author's Collection*)

Raven Meadows, 1962. The development of this area was full of problems and delays. As early as April 1946 the local papers were getting excited about proposals for moving the cattle market out of town and redeveloping the site. The ideal site for the new market was thought to be Harlescott, but by 12 January 1955 the council was still debating the subject, and another four years passed before it opened in Harlescott in April 1959. (*Author's Collection*)

Roushill, 1960. Within a few years of this photograph being taken most of the buildings would disappear. The buildings on the left leading up to Roushill Bank were demolished in the redevelopment of Raven Meadows. The shop belonging to A.G. Thoms, who was listed as a poultry, rabbit and game dealer, was demolished to give wider access between Roushill and Mardol, and the market tower was removed in 1961. There were two public houses on this section of road, the Horseshoes on the corner with the flagpole, and the Sun, two doors further up, with the white strip on the ground floor. The Horseshoes was first recorded in 1861 and it was also known as the Three Horseshoes. It had seven private rooms and three public rooms; its customers were mainly working class. In 1900 Edward Mullard, who lived at Weir Hill, owned it. The Sun had occupied that building since 1828, although another inn of that name had stood on the corner of Mardol and Roushill from about 1780 until the licence was removed to these premises. (*Abbeycolor*)

Roushill, *c.* 1970. In August 1956 Shuker and Son, who had a large garage in Roushill, merged with Charles Clark and Son Ltd. The redevelopment of the area in the late 1960s, with the building of the shopping mall and better road access, gave the firm a chance to build this modern car showroom. It was sited close to the area once occupied by the Sun, but a little further back because of the extra width of the road. As the site was being redeveloped a leading archaeologist, P.A. Barker, excavated part of the old town wall and some interesting pieces of medieval pottery were unearthed. Just above the new showroom is the rear of the newly built Lloyds Bank. (*Abbeycolor*)

Meadow Place, 1960. Meadow Place has also been known as Roushill Walls and Castle Gates Lane. Like the Victoria Inn at the other end of Smithfield Road, the Albert Hotel was first recorded shortly after the opening of the new cattle market, and their names commemorate the Queen and her Consort. For most of the twentieth century the Gough family owned the inn. George Oakley & Co., agricultural implement and tractor dealers, occupied the building on the other corner. They had offices and showrooms in Meadow Place for many years, being ideally sited by the cattle market. The building at the top of Meadow Place, on Castle Gates, was a Congregational church, erected in 1845. When the congregation moved into a new church in Coton Hill this church was adapted into a cinema called the Central Hall. The cinema closed in March 1931 after a fire had destroyed part of the building. (*Abbeycolor*)

Smithfield Road, 1960. The buildings and yard behind the advertising boards was once the timber yard and sawmill belonging to Barker Brothers. The site was taken over by George Phillips, who was listed in 1952 as a marine store dealer. Mr Phillips was known as 'Woppy', which was derived from Whopper, as he was such a big man. The building on the corner at the junction of Chester Street was occupied by William Howe & Sons Ltd, ironmongers and agricultural implement agents. The buildings were later converted into a garage and car showrooms by Charles Clark Ltd. The large grey building in Chester Street is the rear of Chronicle House, the home of the *Shrewsbury Chronicle*. (*Abbeycolor*)

Smithfield Road, 1960. The young men in the crowd always eagerly awaited the carnival float from the Silhouette Factory, as young ladies dressed only in a black body stocking and foundation garments made by the Shrewsbury factory occupied it. During the middle of the 1960s the firm was expanding into new offices, factory and warehouse in Harlescott and opening a new factory in Whitchurch. (*Author's Collection*)

The junction of Smithfield Road and Chester Street, *c.* 1958. J.G. Spence opened an ironmonger's shop in these premises in 1820. William Howe acquired the firm in 1883 and owing to the close proximity of the cattle market he was able to develop the business into other areas, which included being an agent for a wide range of agricultural implements. The building was converted into one of the town's main garages and car showrooms by Charles Clark & Sons Ltd, who renamed the building Austin House as they were the main distributors for Austin motor cars in Shropshire. By the 1960s they were also agents for Riley and the Vanden Plas Princess. They also claimed to be Shrewsbury's leading used car specialists. In the 1930s it was known as Station Garage and was the workshop for the undertaker Edward Owen. (*Author's Collection*)

Chester Street, 1960. In earlier times this street was known as Bagley Bridge, the bridge taking traffic out of town and over the Bagley Brook to Coton Hill. The name is derived from Bokeler, a person who made buckles and who presumably once lived in the area. In the eighteenth century it was known as Back Lane but by 1830 it had acquired its modern name. All the properties on the left from the garage to the brewery have been demolished, as have the cottages on the right. The shop next to the garage belonged to F. Vincent, who was listed as a grocer, fruiterer and confectioner. Next came Watkins's Commercial Hotel, which was run in the 1950s by Mrs R.L. Casewell. (*Abbeycolor*)

Chester Street, 1960. Thomas Hawley founded Southam's Brewery in the early years of the nineteenth century. In about 1852 Thomas Southam, a local wine merchant who wanted to extend his business into brewing beer and other ales, acquired the firm. He had opened a wine and spirits shop on Wyle Cop in 1842. Under his direction the brewery expanded its business and within thirty years owned over twenty public houses in the Shrewsbury area. Southam had a strong sense of public duty and was a borough councillor for forty-four years. He also had the rare distinction of being elected Mayor of Shrewsbury on four separate occasions. This achievement has been commemorated with the naming of the Proud Salopian Inn in Smithfield Road, whose sign bears his portrait in his mayoral robes. In 1983 the brewery was demolished and the site redeveloped into the Gateway Centre. (*Abbeycolor*)

Chester Street, *c.* 1962. This photograph shows Jack Davies in the doorway of his cycle shop during a cleaning up operation after one of the floods of the early 1960s. The machine and the serviceman on the left are both from RAF Shawbury and were one of several units deployed in the town to pump out flooded premises. These warm air-blowing devices were used to dry out the property quickly. The business was started by Mr Davies's father in 1920 and was known as the Castle Cycle Store, selling bicycles, accessories and spares. They also repaired all makes of cycles and guaranteed moderate charges and a quick service. (*Author's Collection*)

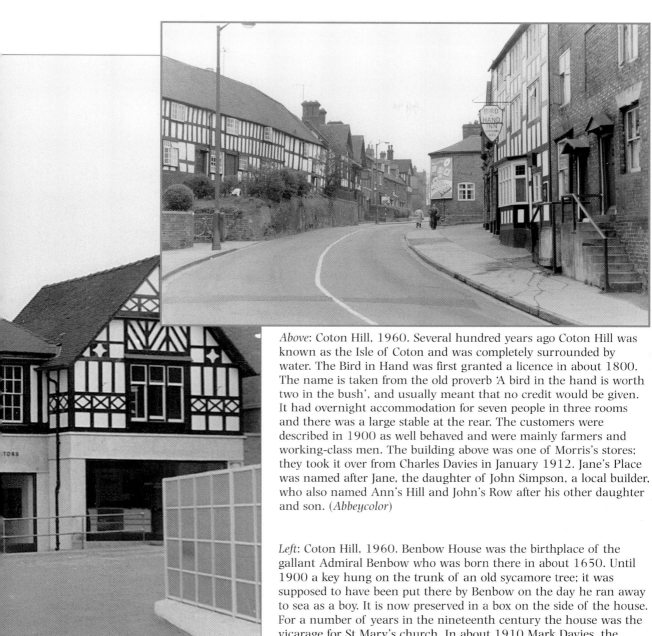

Above: Coton Hill, 1960. Several hundred years ago Coton Hill was known as the Isle of Coton and was completely surrounded by water. The Bird in Hand was first granted a licence in about 1800. The name is taken from the old proverb 'A bird in the hand is worth two in the bush', and usually meant that no credit would be given. It had overnight accommodation for seven people in three rooms and there was a large stable at the rear. The customers were described in 1900 as well behaved and were mainly farmers and working-class men. The building above was one of Morris's stores; they took it over from Charles Davies in January 1912. Jane's Place was named after Jane, the daughter of John Simpson, a local builder, who also named Ann's Hill and John's Row after his other daughter and son. (*Abbeycolor*)

Left: Coton Hill, 1960. Benbow House was the birthplace of the gallant Admiral Benbow who was born there in about 1650. Until 1900 a key hung on the trunk of an old sycamore tree; it was supposed to have been put there by Benbow on the day he ran away to sea as a boy. It is now preserved in a box on the side of the house. For a number of years in the nineteenth century the house was the vicarage for St Mary's church. In about 1910 Mark Davies, the proprietor of a garage on Dogpole, opened another branch in the garden of the house, which was acquired by Furrows in 1919. The name of the firm originates from the furrows ploughed up by Fordson tractors, which Cyril Harrison-Watson, the founder of Furrows, used for a government food production scheme during the First World War. The petrol pumps and the cottages to the left of the building have been removed. (*Abbeycolor*)

Opposite: Coton Hill, 1960. This large timber-framed building, now converted into cottages, was once the great barn belonging to the Mytton family. It is thought that either Thomas or William Mytton built a large mansion here in about 1500, moving from Vaughan's Mansion at the rear of the Square. The mansion, of which nothing remains, would have been perched high up, looking over the river towards Frankwell. Both Thomas and William were Bailiffs of Shrewsbury and ancestors of the notorious Mad Jack Mytton of Halston. At the beginning of the twentieth century an undertaker lived close by and used to display his coffins leaning upright against the wall where the bicycle is parked. Just above is the Royal Oak, which was first recorded from 1804. (*Abbeycolor*)

The junction of Coton Hill, Berwick Road and Ellesmere Road, 1960. The sign on the left directs traffic to Baschurch down the Berwick Road and to Ellesmere straight ahead. The eaves of the new Woodman Inn can be seen above the cottages; it was first recorded as an inn in about 1851 and was later rebuilt. The shop in the centre of the photograph is the grocery shop belonging to the Shrewsbury Industrial Co-operative Society. Behind the wall on the right is Cotonhurst, a fine Victorian house, which was the home of Thomas Corbett, Mayor of Shrewsbury in 1906 and the owner of the Perseverance Iron Works in Castle Foregate. Note the old police box outside the Co-op. (*Abbeycolor*)

Ellesmere Road, 1960. This suburb of Shrewsbury was developed in the nineteenth century when this highway was known as Chester Road. The turning on the right leads into Wood Street, while on the left between the cottages in the centre of the photograph is Elm Street, and beyond the Esso garage on the right is the road leading into Greenfields, an estate laid out in the 1880s. The buildings behind the sleeper fence were part of a large industrial area that contained the Great Western Area Goods Yard, the Great Western Railway Signal & Telegraph Inspector's Office and three railway wagon repair works: the Wagon Repair Ltd, the Central Wagon Co. Ltd and the Doncaster Wagon Co. Ltd. (*Abbeycolor*)

7

Down the Cop

Wyle Cop, 1960. This photograph shows quite clearly the three sections that now make up the Lion Hotel, Shrewsbury's most notable coaching inn on the London to Holyhead Road. The hotel is mentioned as early as 1618 and the oldest part is the timber-framed section that juts out between the brick buildings. From the gallery on the first floor it's believed that the famous Victorian author Charles Dickens 'leant over a queer old rail and looked all down hill and sideways, at the crookedist black and white houses, all of many shapes except straight shapes'. The main building with the impressive doorway and carved lion is reputed to be the work of the architect Thomas Farnolls Pritchard, but the lion and doorway are the work of a local sculptor and were added in 1777. The lower section was incorporated into the hotel at the beginning of the twentieth century, before that part of the building was the local Inland Revenue Office. (*Abbeycolor*)

Wyle Cop, 1960. There are three sections to this street. There is Under the Wyle, the section leading from the English Bridge to the bottom of the hill, the Wyle, the section leading up the bank, and the Cop, which is this area leading from Milk Street to the top of the hill. It is believed the name originates from the Welsh 'hwylfa', a road leading up a hill, and 'coppa', a top or summit, and it is thought that this area at the top of the hill was the first part of the town to be inhabited. The shops to the right of the steps are Paddock's, the furniture, carpet and linoleum specialists, Bradbury's antique shop and H.E. Chatfield's pet shop and ironmongers. Chatfield's had been run for many years by Mr Dickin, also a dairy farmer, who lived in a cottage on the corner of Abbey Foregate and Monkmoor Road. The Ancient Order of Foresters once occupied the rooms above Paddock's shop. (*Abbeycolor*)

The junction of Wyle Cop and Dogpole, 1960. The building at the top of Dogpole is Newport House, now the Guildhall. This was another chemist shop belonging to W.J. Jones, who opened a number of shops in the town in the 1920s. The house is called Warwick House. Before it became a chemist's shop it was a draper's, run by Edward Clarke. Deakin and Cotterill were estate agents, auctioneers and valuers. In 1952 J.P. Wood & Sons from Craven Arms, the famous Chuckie Chicken firm, ran a fruit and vegetable shop there. (*Abbeycolor*)

Wyle Cop, 1960. The frontage of this building was erected in the early 1920s to widen the top of the street after the demolition of a public house known as the London Coffee House from the corner of Dogpole and Wyle Cop. It was designed by A.W. Ward, the Borough Surveyor for over thirty years. He was an admirer of Georgian and Queen Anne architecture and when the opportunity arose for rebuilding in the town he chose these styles, which were more sympathetic to the townscape. A great debt is owed to Ward for preserving and conserving many ancient buildings in the town during his period in office. Preston's carpets and the Midland Wool Shop were there for many years. The rooms above the shop were used by the Refuge Assurance Co. Ltd and as offices by the RSPCA. In 1960 it was possible to leave your bike on the curb, unlocked and unattended, and be sure to find it there when you returned. (*Abbeycolor*)

Wyle Cop, 1960. The timber-framed building just below the Lion Hotel is known as Henry Tudor House as Henry VII is reputed to have lodged there en route from Wales to Market Bosworth, where he beat Richard III and put himself on the throne, heralding the beginning of the magnificent Tudor era. The house was built as one unit with a passageway through the middle of the ground floor. There were shops on the ground floor while the hall was on the first floor. The building also has an unusual coved overhang and a fine traceried window. The small building just below was an inn called the Compasses, a name commemorated in the little shut or passage that runs to the side of the building. (*Abbeycolor*)

Wyle Cop, *c.* 1960. These neo-Georgian frontages are also the work of A.W. Ward and date from the early 1920s when the top of Wyle Cop was widened. Bishop & Brown occupied those premises for around forty years and were able to cater for every need of the photographer from the amateur to the professional. The lady is looking in the window of Evans & Brown, watch and clock makers and jewellers. They were at 13 Wyle Cop for over a hundred years so must have been in the old premises before the alterations. In the 1960s the proprietor of the shop was A.E. Campbell. (*Author's Collection*)

Barrack's Passage, *c.* 1965. This view is taken from Belmont Bank looking towards Wyle Cop and the rear of Henry Tudor House. The timber-framed building is the Lion Tap, a beer house connected to the Lion Hotel. It has also been known as the Trotting Horse and was first licensed in about 1868. The passage was once known as Elisha's Shut as a family of that name lived at the Wyle Cop end. Samuel Elisha and his son Edward were both burgesses of the town and mayors, Samuel in 1725 and Edward in 1743. The modern name arises from the belief that troops were once billeted there for a short while. For a short time the shut was known as Lion Tap Passage. (*J. Savage*)

Wyle Cop, *c.* 1960. This range of properties on Wyle Cop is a wonderful cross section of the variety of architecture you will find throughout the town. The Nag's Head has been recorded as an inn from 1780 although the building is much older. An interesting feature of this building is that the top storey projects several feet over the next floor, but this has been significantly reduced at first-floor level by the insertion of a brick front on the ground floor in Victorian times. The brick building with the parapet, just above the timber-framed building at the foot of the hill is now Tanners Wine and Spirit Merchants. The shopfront is untouched and dates back to the 1820s when shopfronts had to conform to specified standards; looking through the window into the office takes you back to the days of Charles Dickens. (*J. Savage*)

Wyle Cop, 1960. The frontage of this timber-framed house measures 120 ft and was built in about 1460 by Thomas Mytton, a bailiff of Shrewsbury on ten occasions and sheriff of the town in 1483. He was loyal to Richard III and refused Henry Tudor access to the town, swearing that he could only enter over his dead body. He had to save his oath later by lying down at the gates of the old Welsh Bridge and allowing the earl to step over him. This photograph shows two great grocery rivals trading almost next door to one another. On the left is the window of Phillips Stores Ltd, which came to the town in the last quarter of the nineteenth century and opened several stores around the town. Two doors away is Morris's Store, which moved there in 1900. Nearly £300 was spent to refit the shop, which had been a draper and milliner. In 1963 the premises became the first Green Shield Stamp shop in the town, allowing people to choose items in exchange for the books of stamps they had collected. Between the rivals is Bowen's Ltd, who advertised as Value Drapers. They stocked a large selection of ladies' outfits and millinery, general household drapery, carpets, lino, casements and curtain net, dress fabric and silks and men's and boys' clothing. (*Abbeycolor*)

Wyle Cop, 1960. Richard Mansell bought this shop from Miss Annie Williams in about 1890. In 1896 he was listed as a newsagent, bookseller and bookbinder. He also kept a large and varied stock of all kinds of stationery, photo frames, purses, Bibles, prayer and hymn books and story books, which were suitable for presentation. He also kept all kinds of newspapers, periodicals and magazines for sale on the premises, delivery around the town or for postage to any country address. The shop expanded into selling children's toys and was known as the Toy Shop De Luxe, the upstairs floor being transformed into a children's paradise in the weeks before Christmas. As well as running his business Mr Mansell was closely involved with local politics and was Mayor of Shrewsbury in 1934. (*Abbeycolor*)

Wyle Cop, 1960. This is the bottom end of Mytton's Mansion with the original timber frame being hidden by lathe and plaster. Tranquillo Sidoli arrived in Shrewsbury from his native Italy in 1896. He bought his first café in Princess Street from his brother-in-law and was quick to expand throughout the town, opening this café in the 1920s. They are also ice-cream makers, producing a product of the highest quality, and in 1961 they won the coveted Silver Challenge Cup, the highest award in the country for ice-cream making. During the 1960s they also had cafés in the Square, Castle Street and Belstone. If you visited one of their establishments at this time for a coffee, a plate of delicious cream cakes costing 6d each would be brought to your table to tempt you! (*Abbeycolor*)

Wyle Cop, 1960. Even in 1960 Wyle Cop caused problems for motorists, especially when another vehicle parked by the side of the road. During his building of the London to Holyhead Road, Telford wanted to straighten and lower the Cop. He was allowed to reduce the summit by several feet but thankfully the graceful curves of the hill were left intact, preserving the vast history of architecture on both sides of the road. Severe winter weather has also caused problems in the past, especially when the road surface froze and vehicles were unable to negotiate the steep incline. In the early 1960s an electrical heating system was placed under the road to combat the problem, but unfortunately for the motorist it never worked properly and was scrapped. (*Abbeycolor*)

The junction of Wyle Cop and Beeches Lane, 1960. An old Ford Popular and Hillman drive down the Cop towards the English Bridge; the road on the left is Beeches Lane leading on to Town Walls. The lane has nothing to do with beech trees, but is a corruption of Bishop's Lane: the Bishop of Chester owned land in the area in the reign of Edward the Confessor. The building on the left housed the Chinese Laundry run by Chong You; before it became a laundry it was a public house known as the Wherry, first recorded in 1780 and de-licensed on 30 June 1928. From 1828 the carriers' carts from the Ironbridge area used the Wherry as their base. The tall building was once a corn merchant's belonging to A. & H. Attfield, who later moved to Claremont Street. The building is now a restaurant called the Corn House. The Sleep Shop still occupies the building on the junction. At one time it was a confectionery shop belonging to a former Mayor of Shrewsbury, T.P. Deakin. (*Abbeycolor*)

Under the Wyle, 1967. The pile of bricks is all that remain of the old Barge Inn that was first recorded in 1780. It had also been known as the Bridge Inn and had been rebuilt twice. The site was being redeveloped into a garage for Arthur Charles, but later was run by Shrewsbury Motors. In the year 2002 the site is again being redeveloped. The houses are the rear of Marine Terrace, which occupies the old Stone Wharf, once known as Bulgerlode. The houses were once called Stant's Row, after the builder who lived at no. 4. (*Abbeycolor*)

The junction of St Julian's Friars and Beeches Lane, 1960. This cinema was opened as the King's Hall on Thursday 12 March 1914 with the main film being *The Secrets of the Sea*. Prices ranged from 3*d* and 6*d* on the ground floor to 1*s* in the balcony, which had the added attraction of 'courting couple seats', a pair of seats without an arm in the middle. Private boxes could also be hired for 7*s* 6*d*. Sound was introduced to the King's Hall on 1 September 1930, nearly twelve months after the Empire in Mardol had acquired it. In January 1955 it closed for several months while cinemascope was fitted and other alterations were carried out. When it reopened later in the year it had also changed its name to the Century. With the advent of television and the decline in the popularity of the cinema, the Century closed on 10 June 1960, the last film being *Treasure Island* starring Robert Newton. It was reopened for a short time as a bingo hall until the club was transferred to the Granada in 1973. At present the building is under threat of demolition. (*Abbeycolor*)

Town Walls, 1960. This street runs along the largest section of the old town wall to survive and first appears as a street name in 1871. The Catholic cathedral was designed by Edward Welby Pugin and cost in the region of £10,000, of which the Earl of Shrewsbury met part of the cost. The building of the cathedral was not well received by many Protestants, and during the three years of building a great deal of vandalism occurred on the site to try and disrupt the work. The cathedral was officially opened on 29 October 1856 with a High Pontifical Mass sung by Bishop Brown and a sermon preached by Cardinal Wiseman. The cathedral was packed for the event and, on a positive note, many members of the congregation were Protestants. The building with the railings just below the cathedral is St Mary's Catholic school, rebuilt on this site in 1892 to accommodate 260 boys, girls and infants. The school moved from these cramped buildings to a modern building in Castlefields, leaving this site to be redeveloped into luxury town houses. (*Abbeycolor*)

Under the Wyle, *c*. 1960. The Unicorn Hotel has been recorded as an inn since 1780. The building retains many of its original features, though it was extensively modernised in 1884, when one local commented in a newspaper: 'In the case of the most recent vandalism an attempt is being made to imitate the old building; but as the Yankee says, it's not the real grit.' An oak fireplace dated 1603 was uncovered in the assembly room, which is when the building was probably erected. For a short time in 1804 coaches to London, Hereford, Bristol and Chester started from the hotel, but within a few years the coaches had moved to the Lion at the top of the hill and to the Talbot in Market Street. In 1900 the hotel was owned by Shrewsbury and Wem Brewery; it had twenty-three rooms, accommodation for eleven people and stabling for thirty-six horses. The class of customer was considered good, and as well as having a drink they could also enjoy a game of billiards. The hotel closed in 1981 and was turned into a coffee bar, but has since become an Indian restaurant. (*Author's Collection*)

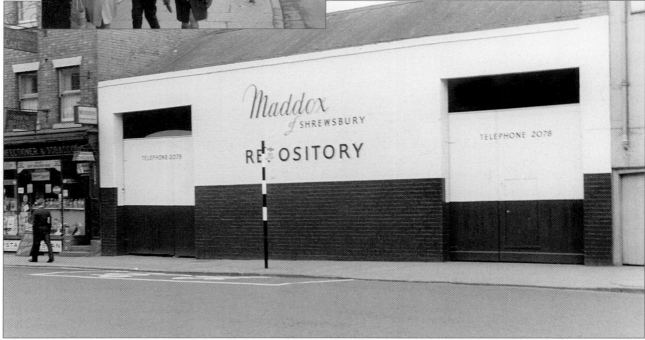

Under the Wyle, 1960. The large building behind this frontage has been used for a variety of purposes. In the late nineteenth century it was the Salvation Army Barracks. Soon after 1900 it was bought for a warehouse by the firm R. Maddox & Co. which had a large department store in the centre of town. The building was used during the Second World War as a mortuary by the United States Air Force, who had a base at Norton Aerodrome near Atcham. In 1965 the warehouse underwent major alterations to be turned into a nightclub called the 7 Club. Tony Connerty, the man behind the venture, spent £8,000 on the conversion. The club was licensed to hold 500 people and was the venue for some of the best groups of the mid-'60s, including The Who, the Barron Knights and the Moody Blues. Mansers' Antique Centre recently occupied the site, until their move last year into an ultra-modern new building in Coleham. (*Abbeycolor*)

Under the Wyle, *c.* 1960. The plans for the reconstruction of the English Bridge, using as much of the original material as possible, were drawn up by A.W. Ward, and work was completed in 1927. These shopfronts were also built several feet further back for wider access on to the new bridge. They were built in the neo-Georgian style and, again, were the work of Arthur Ward. The radio and television sales and service shop belonged to Cyril Chidley, while William Timpson ran the boot and shoe repairer's shop. (*Author's Collection*)

Under the Wyle, 1960. Wales & Edwards opened the garage on the left in March 1927. The garage is built on the site of Sherar's Mansion, built by Thomas Sherar in the middle of the sixteenth century. It was taken over by the Kennings Group, who specialised in Triumph, Jaguar and Daimler motor cars, in 1948. An NCP car park now occupies the site. Just over the English Bridge is the Congregational church with its elegant spire that reaches a height of 115 ft. It was designed by George Bidlake of Wolverhampton and built by Trow & Son of Wednesbury. In 1972, when the Congregational and Presbyterian churches united, it became a United Reform church. (*Abbeycolor*)

St Julian's Friars, 1960. The Franciscan or Grey Friars built their friary here on the banks of the Severn and just outside the town wall in the middle of the thirteenth century. The road leading to the friary has been known by several names, including Fratres Minores in 1246, Bishop Hows Street in 1309 and Dystaffe Lane in 1589. It took its modern name in about 1794 from the simple reason that it was in the parish of St Julian. The poster on the side of the Friar's Fish Café dates the photograph to April 1960 when Emile Ford and the Checkmates were appearing on stage at the Granada. Their greatest hit was 'What do you want to make those eyes at me for', which reached number one in the charts. (*Abbeycolor*)

St Julian's Friars, 1960. The Acorn was first recorded in 1868. In 1901 it was owned by Mrs Annie Johnson, who was also the landlady. It had eight rooms, four private and four for public use. In recent years the inn has been substantially modernised and extended. (*Abbeycolor*)

8

Over the English Bridge

Abbey Foregate, 1960. This view of the Gay Meadow was taken from the rear of the old RSI. Shrewsbury Town Football Club was founded on 20 May 1886. They played all their home matches on the Racecourse at Monkmoor until 1889, when they moved to another pitch in Monkmoor on Ambler's Field. In 1893 they moved their home games to Sutton Lane and two years later to a field in Copthorne opposite the Barracks. In 1910 the club moved to their present pitch at the Gay Meadow, where on 3 September they played their first game against Wolverhampton Wanderers Reserves, losing 2-1. The origin of the name has been lost in history, but what we know today as the Gay Meadow should really be called the Lower Gay, with the Gay Meadow lying higher up the Foregate in the area of Whitehall Street. To the right of the Meadow is Shrewsbury Technical College, built in the 1930s on the site of the old college that was housed in a Georgian building. It became a technical grammar school in 1960 and was renamed the Wakeman in 1965 after Sir Offerley Wakeman, the Chairman of the Governors. (*Abbeycolor*)

Abbey Foregate, 1960. The building of the railway bridge in 1851 across Abbey Foregate completely obscured the view of the Abbey church as you left the town. At first the sides of the bridge were left open, but the smoke and steam and the noise caused by the engines caused so many horses to bolt that the railway company were forced to enclose it. The bridge is a wrought-iron, box girder design. There are three girders, each 63 ft long and 4 ft wide. The whole structure weighs around 96 tons. The bridge was completely overhauled in the 1930s when the attractive wrought-iron railings were added. The tall house on the left was built in about 1850 and belonged to the railway. It was demolished in the late 1960s. The white building on the right was the Bull Inn, the home of a 'convivial club' in the nineteenth century and where Benjamin Disraeli gave a speech to the electors of Shrewsbury when he successfully stood as parliamentary candidate for the town in 1841. The inn's licence was transferred in 1937 to the Harlescott Inn. The Bull became a commercial hotel until it was demolished in 1967. For a short period part of Ratcliff's grocery shop became the Midland Bank. (*Abbeycolor*)

Abbey Foregate, *c.* 1964. The young boys watch with great interest as a resident is rowed by council workers to view his property affected by the flood. The north side of Abbey Foregate is always one of the first areas to be affected and locals will tell you that as the water reaches the mouth of the stone dolphins on the English Bridge the waters of the Severn will spill out of the drains on this side of the road. The building with the four eaves is an almost complete cruck-framed building dating from the fourteenth century. In recent years the whole building has been extensively modernised and turned into a café and restaurant. (*Abbeycolor*)

Abbey Foregate, *c*. 1964. The abbey has seen many floods like this over the years. During the Great Flood of 1795 the *Chronicle* recorded: 'The graves inside the church are sunk in so much that the gravestones are all thrown out of their places. The ends of many of them fallen in and the other ends standing above ground, which makes a most awful and striking appearance and puts us in mind of the general resurrection when it is said the graves shall give up their dead.' On the right a lady walks with great care over the planks that have been laid down for pedestrians, and two council workers manoeuvre their punt towards the flooded houses. Since the severe floods of autumn 2000, flood barriers have been fitted to the doors of the church in the hope of keeping any future flood water out. (*Abbeycolor*)

Abbey Foregate, *c*. 1964. Several severe floods caused a great deal of hardship and disruption in the town during the early 1960s. Perhaps the worst of these were the two floods of December 1965 when the river burst its banks twice in the two weeks before Christmas. The first flood was on Friday 10 December when the river rose at the alarming rate of 3 in per hour to peak on the Saturday at 17 ft 6 in above normal. Sixty council workers were out during the day and thirty at night, using punts and lorries to ferry people, move furniture and deliver meals prepared by the WRVS to marooned householders. Here a council worker prepares to deliver some of the hot dinners of beef stew in these special containers; the service was known as 'Meals on Water Wheels'. The river rose again just eight days after the first flood and marooned householders in their upstairs rooms for another two days. The two disastrous floods caused a great deal of hardship and expense, but the victims were helped by the council who provided them with soap and disinfectant to clean their homes and bags of coal and logs to dry them out. (*Abbeycolor*)

Abbey Foregate, 1960. Abbey House is a fine example of Queen Anne architecture and was erected in about 1698 by Thomas Jenkins, who was Sheriff of Shropshire in 1729. The architect is thought to be a man called Smith from Warwickshire, whose style it resembles. The most striking feature of the house is the wide staircase with its spiral balustrade and large first-floor landing, which allowed sedan chairs to successfully negotiate the corners. The house remained the property of the Jenkins family until 1861 and was later owned by Mrs Lingen–Burton, the wife of a former vicar of the abbey. The house was later owned by the church and for several years was used as the Driving Test Centre, before being sold to Dyke Yaxley & Co., a firm of accountants. (*Abbeycolor*)

Abbey Foregate, *c.* 1960. Until the 1980s this side of Abbey Foregate was the scene of a great deal of industry. On the left is a wagon outside the Abbey station. The line was opened in 1866 as the Potteries, Shropshire and North Wales Railway. Cureton's Garage was opened in the early years of the twentieth century by James Stant, a motor engineer. During the 1930s it became Goode's Garage, run by R.M.W. Jones and C.S. Goode, and was taken over by Cureton's who also had another garage on the other side of the road. Behind the garage was a large petrol depot owned by the Anglo-American Oil Co. Ltd. The man is studying the refectory pulpit that stands isolated in a little garden. (*Abbeycolor*)

Abbey Foregate, *c.* 1955. The two houses on the left were taken down in about 1962 when the site was redeveloped into the town's first Safeway store. Mr Billcliffe lived in the house with the handrails; he was a professional photographer and verger of the abbey for many years. The site was redeveloped again in 2002 with the building of a Netto store. The timber-framed building dates from the sixteenth century and is known as Cold Bath Court. The name refers to a public washing place at the rear of the buildings in the seventeenth and eighteenth centuries. Before 1836 Abbey Foregate ran to the rear of the church and then down the north or right-hand side towards town. The road to the left that cut through a great many of the abbey's domestic buildings was built by Thomas Telford to save a few seconds on his London to Holyhead road. In 1840 the land to the rear of the church was opened as Shrewsbury's first general cemetery. (*Abbeycolor*)

Abbey Foregate, 1960. Only the timber-framed cottages on the left and the Dun Cow Inn on the right remain, the rest having been demolished in the 1960s. At one time there were three schools in this row. The Shrewsbury Collegiate School for Girls was to the left of the cottages. In 1914 the Principal was Miss Prentice who aimed to give the girls in her care 'a thorough education, to train them to become conscientious, unselfish, good women, and to develop their power of character'. In one of the cottages was a small school for young girls run by Miss Ellen Wallett, while in the building to the left of the Dun Cow was Betton House Day and Boarding School for Boys, run by Thomas Stone. Betton House was converted into Betton Garage by Legge and Chamier and was the first garage in the country to provide its customers with a roadside petrol pump. (*Abbeycolor*)

Abbey Foregate, 1960. Fred Pyatt, who was churchwarden of the abbey for many years, rides his bicycle up the old Abbey Foregate. The large building in front of St Mary's spire was erected in about 1842 by Richard Taylor, a local maltster and landowner. In the 1950s and '60s it became known as the Gay Meadow Café and Snack Bar, run by Mrs Bell, and then as Purnell's Café. The almshouses to the left were designed in the Tudor style by Samuel Pountney Smith in 1853. In front they have an open arcade that gives a cloistered effect, and they are built out of red sandstone with a brick dressing, which blends in well with the church. The white house to the right of the café was once the town house of the Hill family from Attingham and was built in about 1510. Before the houses on the extreme right were built it had an open view right up to Whitehall. In about 1828 it became an inn known as the Park, after the public gardens that were laid out to the east and south of the abbey in the eighteenth century. (*Author's Collection*)

Underdale Road, *c.* 1960. The name of this road is derived from 'hundred', an old division of land, and 'hale', a riverside meadow. The Shrewsbury to Wellington Railway line was opened in 1849, splitting this road in two. To overcome the problem a level crossing and footbridge were built at this point, but they caused a great deal of controversy between the railway company and the local residents. Complaints varied from the gates being kept closed for long periods to the footbridge being unsafe for pedestrians. The problem was solved in 1872 after a passing train demolished the footbridge, and this underpass was dug to replace it and the crossing. At the same time that the cutting was dug a gentlemen's urinal was built on the right-hand side. (*Abbeycolor*)

The junction of Abbey Foregate and Monkmoor Road, 1960. This building was once a public house and was recorded as such from 1780 until 1883. The building was owned by the abbey church and was appropriately called the Angel. But by 1883, with the Temperance Movement in full flow, it was thought by many that a church should not own a licensed house, and at a special parish meeting a vote was taken to close the inn. It later became a lodging house known as Monkmoor Lodge, but in recent years has been completely refurbished and divided into flats. In 1960 the first shop in Monkmoor Road was an upholsterer's run by Mr Evans. (*Abbeycolor*)

Crowmere Road to Belvidere Road, *c.* 1955. The photographer has his back to Abbots Road and is looking over the open site, now occupied by St Winifred's Catholic church, to the steel houses in Caradoc Crescent. German prisoners of war carried out the drainage system and other preparatory work before they were repatriated. These houses were prefabricated and were built in reverse, starting with the roof and then filling in the gaps. They were a temporary measure and it was hoped to replace them within a few years with modern bungalows, but this never happened and many are now owner occupied, have been completely renovated and some given a stone cladding. Before the Catholics built their church on this site the Church of England hoped to erect a church there, moving from St Peter's on Monkmoor Road, which would be used as a parish hall. On two Rogation Sundays a procession took place from St Peter's church to the site. It was led by the Salvation Army Band and was followed by a farm wagon borrowed from Mr J. Overy. This was full of hay that was placed on the green before a short Rogation service was held, laying claim to the site. Both the Archdeacon of Salop and the Bishop of Shrewsbury were in favour of the scheme, but the vicar of the abbey, the Revd M.L.A. Wilkinson, was not. (*Author's Collection*)

Abbey Foregate, 1960. This view of Lord Hill's Column was taken from Wenlock Road towards the new Shirehall site. The building to the left of the column is Column Lodge, the home of the caretaker to the monument. Sergeant Davies was the first to hold that position and was given the post at the express wish of Lord Hill, whom he had served with in both the Peninsula Wars and at Waterloo. The statue of Lord Hill was modelled by Panzetta and made by Coade and Sealy in their artificial Coade stone. The figure of Lord Hill is 17 ft tall and cost £449, which also included fitting it at the top of the column. Unfortunately for his lordship the Coade stone has not weathered well and over the years a great deal of money has been spent restoring the statue. In 1945 one of his arms fell off and twenty years later, when there was another crisis, a proposal to replace the figure with a glassfibre copy was seriously considered. The statue was completely overhauled in 1993. (*Abbeycolor*)

Abbey Foregate, 1964. In May 1945 the council published far-reaching plans to redevelop the top of Abbey Foregate into the main civic and administrative area of the town. The eminent architect Sir Percy Thomas was engaged to draw up the blueprint for a new Shirehall, police station and county hospital with room for 1,000 patients, along with car parks, recreation grounds and service roads for other public buildings such as fire and ambulance stations. Throughout 1946 there were a number of attacks on the scheme and a protest meeting was held in June 1946 that condemned the whole plan. However, in 1959 the *Chronicle* announced: 'Salop to press on with the Column Scheme at Shrewsbury'. By 1963 the plans had been passed and Sir Offley Wakeman laid the foundation stone in July 1964. This photograph was taken from the column and shows the fan-shaped foundations of the Council Chamber and the main buildings in the background. The new building was never popular and in April 1965 was slated as 'that expensive monstrosity'. (*Author's Collection*)

9

Coleham &
Belle Vue

Longden Coleham, 1960. There was a settlement in this area in Saxon times but the origin of the name is uncertain. This area of town was greatly affected by industry in the nineteenth century and many courts and rows of houses sprang up to accommodate the workers. In this row of houses in 1896 there were several railwaymen, who worked as cleaners, firemen, platelayers and drivers. At the far end there was a grocer called Alfred Davies and a hairdresser by the name of Webb. The white building at the bottom of the street is the Seven Stars, first recorded in 1785. There were once two inns of that name in Coleham standing close to each other, but the second one had gone by 1820. A brass plaque was once screwed to the wall over the fireplace in the Seven Stars. It read: 'To our very great surprise, the Severn to this place did rise. Anno. 1796.' It recorded the height of the Great Flood of that year. (*Abbeycolor*)

Moreton Crescent, 1960. This road was once part of Belle Vue Road but was renamed in 1932 after Moreton Villa, the home of John Hazledine, son of William Hazledine and Mayor of Shrewsbury in 1855. The shop on the right was for many years a fish and chip shop until it was demolished in the 1970s; the site was left open as a little rose garden. In the nineteenth century it was known as Cocoa House, a temperance alternative to the many public houses in the area, and a place to relax and meet your friends. (*Abbeycolor*)

Old Coleham, 1960. This would have been the main road out of town to Meole Brace before Moreton Crescent was built in the middle of the nineteenth century. Coleham Garage was known as Carline Motor Works and was run by Mr Strefford before being taken over by James Owen, a motor engineer. During the 1960s J. & D. Motors, the second-hand car and boat specialists, occupied the site. The large building on the right was the home of Andrew Casserley, the haulage and removal contractor. It was then occupied by W.R. Pugh, the undertakers, before being demolished in December 1978 to make way for Anthony Horton's new showroom. The cottages met a similar fate during the late 1960s. (*Abbeycolor*)

Longden Coleham, 1960. The cottages on the left are 30 to 36 Longden Coleham. They were flooded by the Severn on a regular basis and were replaced in the late 1960s by modern houses built above the flood plain. The Hen and Chickens public house was first recorded in 1856 in an old timber-framed building on that site and was attached to Trouncer's Brewery at the top of the road. The two alleys on either side of the inn are School Close and School Lane, both leading to Trinity school. During the last century the shop on the corner of School Lane was first a grocer's shop and then a fried fish merchant's. (*Abbeycolor*)

Longden Coleham, 1960. In this view we are looking in the opposite direction to the last photograph, with the Hen and Chickens on the right. The white building in the centre is another inn called the Cross Foxes. It was first licensed in 1883 and like the Hen and Chickens still survives today. Just below the Cross Foxes is the Mission Room, built by the congregation of Holy Trinity church on Belle Vue in 1905. On the left is part of the frontage belonging to W.R. Pugh the undertaker; at the beginning of the last century it was an outlet for the Shrewsbury Industrial Co-operative Society. The building with the cone-shaped turret on the roof is the pumping station, built in 1900 to pump sewage up to the sewage farm at Monkmoor. (*Abbeycolor*)

Longden Coleham, 1960.
C. Flower's shop was on the bend of the road near the junction of Coleham Head, on land now occupied by the Carline Fields housing complex. The shop was listed as a general store, but seemed to sell mainly cigarettes and confectionery, and was typical of so many shops in the suburbs of the town. There had been a shop on this site since the nineteenth century. In about 1900 they renumbered Longden Coleham, with this house being changed from 129 to 165. (*Abbeycolor*)

Longden Coleham, 1960. Up until the mass slum clearance schemes of the 1960s most of the suburbs of the town were self-sufficient, supplying the residents with all the shops and services they needed. In 1895 the newsagent's was a tobacconist and sub-post office run by M.A. Evans; it became a newsagent's in the 1930s. In the 1960s it was Domestic Supplies, run by Margaret and Jock Love. The shop to the right was once occupied by J.E. Watkins, a monumental mason, but by 1905 it had become a newsagent and by 1929 a confectionery shop run by a Miss Eliza Taylor. W. Sankey's shop sold grocery and hardware, but for many years Samuel Taylor, a tobacconist and pipe maker who had taken the business over from his father, occupied it. In 1882 the passageway to the left was called Pipe Passage, after Mr Taylor's trade of making clay pipes, but towards the end of the nineteenth century the name was changed to Fairford Place. (*Abbeycolor*)

Longden Coleham, 1960. This view is looking up towards Longden Road and the two chimneystacks of Trouncer's Brewery. A sale notice in 1828 stated that the brewery was capable of brewing 120 barrels of beer daily and had eight vats that could hold 1,700 barrels. The brewery also boasted a convenient wharf with barges loaded daily for Coalbrookdale, Bewdley, Worcester, Gloucester and Bristol. The modern shops on the right were built in about 1935 and housed Mrs Mound's fancy repository, Mrs Allen's wardrobe shop and Kenneth Rowland's greengrocery. The old buildings on the left were removed to make way for Jack's Fish Saloon and Restaurant, which moved just across the street from the approach road to the Greyfriars Bridge. The shop next door belongs to the Shrewsbury Co-op, which opened in about 1932. The road to the left is Greyfriars Road, built in about 1914. (*Abbeycolor*)

Longden Road, 1960. Luciefelde House was built in the nineteenth century on the corner of Longden Road and Kingsland Road. It was the home of Thomas Trouncer who had bought the brewery just below his home in 1845. He became Mayor of Shrewsbury in 1860 and was re-elected for a second term the following year. In 1938 the house was converted into an inn called the Pengwern and the licence from the Three Tuns in Longden Coleham was transferred there when the old inn closed. The Pengwern closed in 1997 and was demolished to make way for Pengwern Court, a complex of homes for senior citizens. (*Author's Collection*)

Shrewsbury sheds, *c.* 1955. This is a view of the old LMS sheds with three engines. The one on the left is an Ivatt Class Two; these engines were nicknamed 'Mickey Mouse' by drivers. The centre engine is a 'Black' Five, which were the workhorses of their day and popular with the drivers. This one is a later Stanier design model that had been modified by H.G. Ivatt, the designer of the first locomotive. The engine on the right is a British Rail Class Four tank engine. With the demise of steam the area fell derelict until the opening of the new gyratory system in 1991, giving easier access and breathing new life into the area with the opening of a supermarket, cinema complex, fast food outlets and a pub and restaurant, as well as a variety of sale rooms and offices. (*Author's Collection*)

Shrewsbury sheds, *c.* 1955. The engine is a British Railways 'Black' Five, passing the Sutton Bridge Junction signal box and heading towards Hereford. The line directly behind the signal box is the old Severn Valley Line, which was known to the drivers as the Holiday Line. The building on the right is the canteen, now the Reabrook Social Club, while the large building behind is the LMS Barracks. The tall building in the centre to the left of the chimneys is one of the GWR offices, known as the Top Office. Directly below the office and chimneys is the roofline of the GWR locomotive sheds, while on the extreme left is a gasometer. (*Author's Collection*)

10

Over the Welsh Bridge

Frankwell, *c.* 1962. This view was taken from the top of the multi-storey car park in Bridge Street during the flood of that year. The buildings immediately below are parts of Morris's office and warehouse complex. The large building to the left of the Welsh Bridge belongs to Hall, Wateridge & Owen Ltd. The auctioneers and estate agents had recently moved into the building that had once been a warehouse occupied by Richard Bromley, the seed and corn merchant. The small building to the left is part of T. Birch & Co.'s skin yard at the rear of the Fellmonger's Hall. To the right of the bridge is the corrugated-iron building of the Frankwell Forge. The house above the forge, with eighteen windows, housed the Anchor public house, while the new building to the right of the inn is Kwik's supermarket. It was demolished in 1995 and flats now occupy the site. (*Author's Collection*)

Frankwell Quay, 1960. The Quay was built in 1608, the year after Mardol Quay was opened. The open car park was once a warren of houses and passages known as White Horse Court, Severn Square, St George's Buildings and Stew Cottages. The name Stew recalls the fishpond belonging to the medieval St George's Hospital that stood close by, and the cottages at the rear are all that remains of Severn Square. The building on the corner is the Anchor Inn, first recorded in 1780. In 1900 the landlady was Mary Drayton, who is said to have kept a fair house and whose customers were made up from the working classes, hawkers and dealers. The Downes family ran the grocer's shop to the left for many years. It was taken over by Tommy Cartwright, who also ran a newsagent further up Frankwell. The building next to the shop was once Mr Forrest's Mission Room. (*Abbeycolor*)

Frankwell, 1960. This flood occurred in December 1960 and was the first of a number of severe floods that would affect the town in the first seven years of that decade. The building on the left was still occupied by Richard Bromley, the seed merchant, while just beyond are the new flats and maisonettes built above the flood line on Natty Prices Corner in 1960. Behind the frontage of the white shop is an old timber-framed building; the left-hand section was once the barber's shop belonging to Ted Millington. The timber-framed building with its extensive frontage was originally built as one dwelling and dates from the sixteenth century. Mr Eldred, the owner of Eldred Mottram & Co., tent and marquee manufacturers, tarpaulin and rope and twine makers, skilfully renovated the building. The business was established in 1790 on several sites around the town. The house to the right of the large gates was another grocery shop, this one belonging to Florrie Wainwright. (*Abbeycolor*)

Frankwell, 1960. The main street leading from the Welsh Bridge towards Wales was known in medieval times as Frankvile. One explanation for the name is that it comes from an old French word meaning a free town, a place where two hostile races; here the English and Welsh could meet and trade. Another interpretation is that shortly after the Norman Conquest forty-five French-speaking traders set up their own community, calling it Frankville, a settlement outside the jurisdiction of the town and free of taxes and tolls. The wealth of timber-framed houses is indicated by those on the right; the majority of the buildings above are also timber-framed but were encased in a brick skin when timber went out of fashion. The houses fronting the main street are built on the old burgage plots, long narrow strips of land running off at right angles from the main street. (*Abbeycolor*)

Frankwell, *c.* 1965. Until it was removed in about 1970 this was undoubtedly the finest timber-framed building in Frankwell. It was built by John Worral between 1676 and 1677 on the site of an older dwelling, inhabited by Lewis Thomas, the first Suffragan Bishop of Shrewsbury. In the eighteenth century it became an inn, first licensed as the Royal Oak and then the Cross Keys. The name was changed again in about 1828 to the String of Horses. The inn was delicensed in 1907 and was redeveloped into a grocer's shop owned by the Shrewsbury Co-operative Industrial Society. Unfortunately during the alterations a great deal of oak panelling was removed and an 8 ft wide oak fireplace with an ornamental brick cornice and wide brick chimney were also taken down. Before the inn was delicensed the frontage on either side of the arch was a grocer's shop run by George Stealey. The Co-op then occupied all the building up to the arch, with the shop to the right of the arch becoming the London Central Meat Co. Ltd butcher's shop. It ended its days as a ladies' hairdressing salon called the Tudor Rose. The building was re-erected at Avoncroft Museum near Bromsgrove. (*Author's Collection*)

Frankwell, 1962. This photograph was taken on 15 June, the day Tommy Davies retired as a chimney sweep. He was a well-liked figure in and around Frankwell, and even before the advent of the vacuum cleaner he was well known for his cleanliness and would remove every speck of soot before he left. Local children would wait with great excitement for his early arrival, which was always by bike with his brushes and rods strapped to the cross bar. As he swept the chimney the children would be sent outside to watch for the brush emerging through the top of the pot. By the 1960s, with households moving from coal fires to electric and gas, sweeps were not in demand, and at the time of his retirement Mr Davies was unable even to give his business away. (*Author's Collection*)

Copthorne Road, 1960. John Drayton, a Primitive Methodist lay preacher, opened his wheelwright shop in these premises in the middle of the nineteenth century. By the 1890s he had become an undertaker and had established a livery stable there. By 1917 Harry Perry had taken the business over, and in 1935 he was advertised as a funeral director and furnisher, and a motor hearse and coach proprietor. By the early 1950s a garage had been established there, and the funeral parlour was being run by Frank Painter. Towards the end of the 1950s Frank Painter moved his business to Spring Gardens and the garage was taken over by the Green brothers. The man in the white overall is Freddy Green, who was in charge of the petrol pumps. (*Abbeycolor*)

New Street, 1960. In this view the photographer is looking back towards the junction with Copthorne Road. The open space on the right is the site of Maddox's Buildings. The houses on the left with verandas are quite substantial Victorian houses. The main living rooms are on the level of the veranda with the bedrooms on the next two floors. The area under the veranda is below ground level at the rear and was used as a scullery and washhouse. Just beyond the cottages part of Pengwerne House School can be seen. It started in the nineteenth century as a ladies' school run by Miss Pritchard when the house was known as Olive Cottage. The school took pupils aged five to eleven and eventually moved to new premises in Copthorne, and this house became a private dwelling once again. The house in the centre with the porch is part of Millington's Hospital and the building to the right with the signboard is the Cross Guns Inn, demolished a few years later for the construction of the Frankwell island. (*Abbeycolor*)

The junction of New Street and Copthorne Road, 1960. New Street is first shown on Rocque's map of 1746. In the past parts of the street were known as Slah Street, derived from the sloe tree, and may have incorporated parts of Copthorne. Norton's Lane was a name used for part of the road during the early eighteenth century. Charlie Wilding, a well-known Shropshire athlete, occupied the house on the junction. His best event was the high jump in which he was Midland County Champion on several occasions. The open space on the left was caused by the demolition of Maddox's Buildings. They were built by John Maddox, a maltster who lived at Quarry View House. Many of the houses were built back to back, had communal toilets and no running water. Even so, when eviction notices were served on people living there in April 1959, several families refused to leave their homes at first. (*Abbeycolor*)

New Street, 1960. This section of the street leading to Porthill was known in 1838 as Boat House Lane. Behind the sandstone wall are three houses, Priory Vista, The Glimpse and The Retreat, built in about 1930 on old garden plots. In the garden of the Retreat is a very nice summerhouse that was built in the eighteenth century. The garden on the right is part of a nursery, founded by Oscar Prichard in 1857 on land that once extended down to the foot of Porthill. Mr Prichard also had a nursery at Netley Hall and a shop in the Market Arcade. He sold his New Street Nursery to the Council in May 1947. The house behind the street lamp is Yew Tree Villa, in 1961 it was converted into luxury retirement flats. The large white house at the bottom of the street is Severn Lodge. It was built in the Gothic style in the early part of the nineteenth century and was once the home of the Revd J.H. Charters, a member of the Shrewsbury Schools Board and a manager of St George's School. Princess Anne stayed there during the 1960s while visiting the town for a twenty-first birthday party. (*Abbeycolor*)

Frankwell, 1960. This view is looking up Frankwell towards the Mount. The white building in the centre is the Buck's Head Inn, which was first recorded in 1835. In 1851 James Birch was landlord, and to supplement his income he was also a blacksmith, plying his trade in the yard at the rear. All the buildings on the left up to the Buck's Head were demolished for the construction of Frankwell traffic island. The house just above the timber-framed cottages was for a short time an inn called the Golden Lion, recorded from 1851 to 1883. On the opposite side of the road is another inn called the Swan. Records show that there was an inn of that name in Frankwell from as early as 1657, but its site is unknown; first records of this building being used as the Swan date from about 1871. In 1900 the inn had ten rooms, seven private and three public. There were also four stables at the rear that had been let to Arthur Rowson, a glass stainer, as workshops. For entertainment at the inn you could play bagatelle. (*Abbeycolor*)

11
Below the Castle

Castle Gates, 1960. The castle was built overlooking Shrewsbury's most vulnerable point, the only land route into town. The first stone building was introduced during the reign of Henry II, who built the inner bailey and first hall. In the reign of Edward I the hall was enlarged and the distinctive rounded towers were added. After years of neglect Thomas Telford restored the building as a home for Sir William Pultney who was member of parliament for the town. In 1924 the Shropshire Horticultural Society bought it for the town, with the main hall being transformed into a Council Chamber. In 1985 it gained a new lease of life as the town's new Regimental Museum, when military historian Geoffrey Archer Parfitt combined the museums of the KSLI, the Royal Horse Artillery and the Shropshire Yeomanry, and brought them under one roof. He became the museum's first curator and had the unenviable job of trying to salvage his life's work after the IRA bombed the castle in 1992. The two brick buildings below housed a barber's shop on the left and a jeweller's run by Charles Grove on the right. For many years the timber-framed building was a confectionery shop and dining rooms run by Jacob Davies. Morris's bought him out in 1919 when they purchased the business and the Bull's Head Inn next door for £7,500. (*Author's Collection*)

Castle Gates, 1960. The photographer is looking towards Castle Foregate and the junction of Chester Street on the left. The building on the immediate right was built as a Congregational church before becoming a cinema. The shop next door belonged to Mr Gibbs, a local butcher. The Castle Vaults was first recorded in 1829, while the Bull's Head just two doors away was opened three years later in 1832. The Bull was once the dropping-off point for carriers arriving in the town from Hawkstone, High Ercall and other areas to the north. The ornate building in the centre was once a temperance hotel called the Welcome Coffee Palace, or just the Welcome, before changing its name to the Cleveland Hotel. It was a commercial and family hotel and restaurant and guaranteed first-class accommodation for cyclists at reasonable rates, but to be sure of securing a bed it was best to write in advance. Small parties could also be provided with dinner or tea at short notice. The building was taken over by Richard Mansell in the 1920s and turned into a wholesale newspaper, magazine and stationery outlet. (*Abbeycolor*)

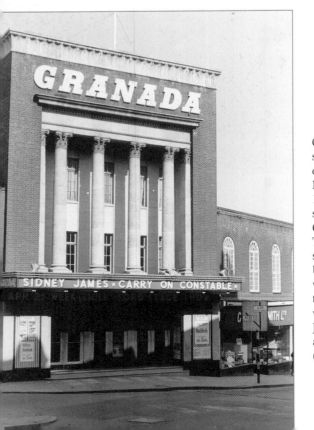

Castle Gates, 1960. The Granada was built in the early 1930s on the site of the old Station Hotel. The exterior was thought to be the work of Cyril Masey, the architect of the Granada at Tooting. The Mayor, Mrs Marion Wallace Cock, carried out the opening ceremony on 14 November 1934; the opening film was *The Camels Are Coming*, starring Jack Hulbert and Anna Lee. On 6 December 1954 Cinemascope was introduced to the town with the film *The Robe*. Throughout its life the cinema hosted many live shows, and with seating for over 1,000 it was also a magnificent theatre venue. Unfortunately, with the decline of the cinema in the early 1970s it was decided to close the bingo hall at the Century and move the club to the Granada. The cinema closed on Saturday 31 March 1973, with the final film being the *Valachi Papers* starring Charles Bronson. Just over two weeks later on 17 April 1973 the building was opened as a bingo hall, which it still remains but now called the Gala. (*Abbeycolor*)

Castle Foregate, 1960. Cleveland House, the wholesale stationery warehouse for R. Mansell & Sons, is on the left. The business was taken over by Surridge & Dawson, but when they moved the business out to the Battlefield Enterprise Park the building was converted into Connoisseur Bespoke Furnishers. On the far right is Chronicle House, which was opened in 1927 and is the home of Shrewsbury's oldest weekly newspaper. It was founded by Thomas Wood and the first issue appeared on 23 November 1772, priced at 2d. To the left of Chronicle House is the ornate frontage of the Station Hotel. It was first recorded as the Grapes in 1828 and at one time a fine carved sign of a bunch of grapes hung outside. It changed to its present name in 1939 after the old Station Hotel had been demolished and the site redeveloped into the Granada cinema complex. The railway bridge was altered in March 1962 when the arch was replaced by a straight girder bridge designed at Paddington. Note the street furniture on the right: a pair of old traffic signals, a police box and a telephone booth, with a post box and stamp vending machine at the rear. (*Abbeycolor*)

Castle Foregate, 1960. The photographer has his back to the railway bridge and is looking up towards Castle Gates. Before being incorporated into Mansell's warehouse the building to the left of the Station Hotel was occupied by S. Edwin Corbett, an agricultural engineer. The business extended through from Castle Foregate to Chester Street. In 1935 he was advertised as a manufacturer of cheese presses, curd mills, ploughs and horse hoes, and as an agent for all leading farm implement manufacturers. Just above and to the right of the bus is the Granada complex and above that, on the corner of Meadow Place, is another of the National Milk Bars. The timber-framed building just below the library is part of Blower's Repository, built by J. & B. Blower in 1902 when they removed their house furnishing and removal business from Butcher Row. The business was sold to W.H. Smout & Son. (*Abbeycolor*)

Shrewsbury station, *c.* 1962. The engine standing at number six bay is the *County of Dorset* about to move off on a line towards Wolverhampton. The steam emitted from the front stack indicates that the driver is just holding or blowing the brake off. At one time an iron and glass roof had covered the whole of the station. Part of the northern end was replaced in 1924 by canopies after it had become unsafe. Problems had arisen as early as 1887 when part of this section had collapsed under the weight of snow and had killed a passenger waiting on the platform. In 1961 British Rail began a massive overhaul of the station, which included the removal of the old roof and its replacement with new platform shelters. In this photograph some of the girders are still in place but the platforms are open to the elements. (*Author's Collection*)

Shrewsbury station, 11 January 1965. This was the worst rail accident the town had seen since the disaster of November 1907. The crash occurred at 5.45 a.m. when a diesel-hauled freight train from Saltney to Pontypool Road left the line and crashed into the Coton Hill South signal box, completely destroying the box and killing the signalman. The 114-ton train was carrying explosives, animals, limestone hydrochloric acid and caustic soda. Six heifers were killed in the crash and another was later put down. The fumes from the acid and the caustic soda mixed to cause pungent fumes and people living in the area were warned to keep their windows shut. Firemen wearing breathing apparatus took over an hour to find the signalman's body and another hour to release him. The driver of the diesel was also trapped, and after being released underwent a three-hour operation at the RSI for severe arm, leg and head injuries. The fireman in the cab had a miraculous escape, walking away from the accident with just a minor hand injury. (*Author's Collection*)

Howard Street, 1960. This street has been known in the past as Terrace Walk and Castle Hill. With the building of the railway station on the right in 1848, the area was greatly altered. The modern name commemorates John Howard, the great prison reformer, whose bust in a canopied niche can be seen over the main doors into the prison. Part of the Butter Market, built in 1835, can be seen on the skyline. It was once the terminus of the Shrewsbury Canal until taken over by the railway as a warehouse in 1857. The timber-framed building was one of the properties used by the electrical firm of A.R. Mitchell. The buildings on the corner had been occupied by George Oakley's works. (*Abbeycolor*)

Howard Street, 1960. The street was once straight but was re-aligned during the alterations and enlargements to the railway station at the beginning of the twentieth century. The large building just above the railway bridge is one of the goods sheds in the GWR yard and cattle loading station. In the 1950s local coal merchants W.J. Gregory, S. Pugh and A. Wassall all had offices there. The buildings on the right have been demolished and the site redeveloped into the Royal Mail sorting office. (*Abbeycolor*)

Wharf Road, Castle Foregate, 1960. This short road leads to the Shrewsbury Canal. It was soon to disappear when the Royal Mail buildings on the left and the property on the right were redeveloped into a new postal sorting office. The new building also spoilt this view of Shrewsbury Prison from Castle Foregate. The prison stands at the top of the bank overlooking the river. It was designed by John Hiram Haycock and incorporated many of John Howard's up-to-date ideas. Thomas Telford built it between 1787 and 1793 and he is believed to have designed the gatehouse. As late as 1935 Wharf Road was occupied by an ironmonger, two coal merchants, a haulier and several cottages. (*Abbeycolor*)

Castle Foregate, 1960. Castle Foregate was once known as North Foregate, and the name referred to the whole area, not just the road leading out of town, which in earlier times was called Haughmond Street. The building on the right is the Royal Mail sorting office. For many years the Fawcett family ran the newsagent on the left of the main gate of the Great Western goods yard, while Ernest Suter, a radio and electrical engineer, occupied the cottages to the right. The tall building is the Rock and Fountain Inn, which was first recorded as a beer house in 1879 but not named until 1883. The name alludes to the legends where the blood of a saint has been spilt on a rock and miraculously a spring or fountain of healing water has sprung from that barren spot. Like the other suburbs of the town, Castle Foregate was full of houses without the basic sanitary needs, many of them in cramped courts and alleys. Vere Place in particular was so unhealthy that in the middle of the nineteenth century it was known as Typhus Place. (*Abbeycolor*)

Castle Foregate, 1963. The Royal Mail sorting office was built on this site at the beginning of the twentieth century. Until the move to Castle Foregate mail had been sorted at the main post office on Pride Hill, but this site was thought ideal because of the close proximity of the railway station. On the right are the loading bays, which were built to face the main road, but with the growth of traffic, near a busy junction, had by the 1960s become a hazard. Within a few years of this photograph the frontage was demolished and a new office was built on the site, which also incorporated the land on the junction of Howard Street. In the early 1980s over £2 million was spent extending the office to the left and making it into a modern automated complex ready for the twenty-first century. (*Abbeycolor*)

Castle Foregate, 1960. The garage and the mock-timber building on the right were the two properties that were swallowed up in the 1980s extension to the sorting office. Between 1871 and 1883 the garage was a public house called the Crown; it then became a fried fish shop run by Joseph Tonks in 1896 before Alfred Doody opened his cycle shop there. In 1874 John Rainford, a cabinetmaker, opened his workshop next door. He advertised as an upholsterer, coffin maker and general undertaker, guaranteeing workmanship and materials of the best quality. R.S. Hughes, a motor engineer, converted both buildings into the Castle Foregate Motor Co. garage in the 1920s. In 1935 the business was taken over by the John Whalley Organisation who also controlled Furrows, James' Garage in Dorrington and Deemster Investment Trust Ltd. To the left of the nearer arch is the Britannia Inn, which was formerly known as the Engine and Tender, and just two doors further up the street was the Bell Inn, recorded between 1883 and 1925 and owned by the Holt family. (*Abbeycolor*)

Castle Foregate, 1960. The Shrewsbury Industrial Co-operative Society first moved into Castle Foregate in about 1893 next door to the Bell Inn, but by 1915 they had moved into these purpose-built premises. By the 1920s the company had retail outlets in all the main suburbs of the town. The Crown and Anchor used to be owned by Southam's Brewery. It was first recorded as a public house in 1828 and for a short period in the 1860s and '70s it was the meeting point for carriers to Hadnall and Rodington. (*Abbeycolor*)

Castle Foregate, 1960. The building on the left with the magnificent clock tower is Thomas Corbett's Perseverance Iron Works. When the firm was established in the middle of the nineteenth century it was the most up-to-date works in the country, producing a wide variety of agricultural equipment including ploughs, harrows, drills, scarifiers and rollers. Two of Mr Corbett's machines were singled out for special praise, his Eclipse, a combined winnowing, corn and seed dressing machine, and a new combination winnower, corn elevator and weighing machine, which between them brought him 153 royal and international first prizes at agricultural shows around the world. Mr Corbett died in 1917 but the works continued until 1927. The buildings were bought by Morris & Co. in 1929 for £6,500 for the relocation of their oil works. The site has been the scene of two fires, the first in 1905 when damage was estimated at over £8,000, and again in 1954 when a great deal of damage was done to the front of the building, but fire crews prevented the blaze reaching the production areas. (*Abbeycolor*)

New Park Road, 1960. This stretch of road was officially part of New Park Road, but was known locally as Gas House Lane, owing to the close proximity of the gas works on the left. The Shrewsbury Gas Light Co., founded in 1820, occupied an extensive area at this junction. At one time there were three gasometers at the rear, the largest holding 750,000 cu. ft of gas. In 1932 a carbonising plant was opened, which was capable of carbonising 80.4 tons of coal a day, producing 1,460,000 cu. ft of gas. The front of the building facing St Michael Street was built out of Ruabon brick with an ornamental dressing. Unfortunately in recent years the building has been reduced to one storey, but some of the Victorian frontage still survives in the Fitness First Centre. The opening before the road narrows is the entrance to Coal Wharf Square, while the terraced houses at the top lead round to Beacall's Lane. (*Abbeycolor*)

New Park Road, *c.* 1960. All the buildings on this photograph were demolished in the early 1960s. The terrace of houses on the left ran from the turn to the Canal Tavern to Lime Tree House. The white building in the centre is another of Morris's grocery shops, which the firm acquired from W. Yates in 1900. The shop was completely refitted with mahogany units, gas lighting and blinds. Mr Yates was retained as the new shop manager. The building on the right is the Wesleyan chapel, built on New Park Road between Beacall's Lane and North Street in 1837. (*Abbeycolor*)

New Park Road, 1960. The name of this road recalls the new part of the deer park belonging to the Earl of Shrewsbury. Until the council took control in 1858 it was a private road. Its modern name appears in an 1861 directory. The first road on the left is Argyll Street and the second is John Street. The building running between them is the Gospel Hall, which has been a place of worship for over a hundred years. Across the road there are two sets of terraced houses running off at right angles. The first is Poplar Avenue and the second is Stanley Terrace, and just beyond is the Bowling Green Inn, which was first mentioned in 1861. (*Abbeycolor*)

Queen Street, Castlefields, 1950. Alan and Dorothy Reynolds are seen here in the workshop at the rear of their house making homemade sweets. Alan was wounded in a bayonet charge with the Grenadier Guards during the Second World War. The wound left him completely blind and he was transferred to the temporary St Dunstan's Home at Church Stretton where he met Dorothy. Moving to Shrewsbury he became a telephonist, but in the evenings after work he would make sweets for the local children. Within two years he was making more than forty different types of sweet ranging from acid drops, toffees and butterscotch to chocolate animals and figures. (*Author's Collection*)

During the day there was a constant knocking at the door and Dorothy was kept very busy serving children and adults who, after trying Alan's sweets, would eat no others. They kept jars of sweets, on the stairs and on a table in the hall, and smiling children from all over the neighbourhood would bring their pennies and sweet coupons to buy the nicest sweets they had ever tasted. Soon the couple acquired a shop in the Market Hall, which offered their wares to a wider range of customers, and today there are many fifty to sixty year olds who remember with great affection the couple who brought smiles to their faces all those years ago. (*Author's Collection*)

12
Around the River Severn

The Welsh Bridge, 1960. This bridge was erected several yards downstream from the old medieval bridge. It was designed and built by two Shrewsbury architects and builders Carline and Tilley. It cost £8,000 and has five semi-circular arches topped by an ornamental balustrade and is 266 ft long and 30 ft wide. The arch on the Frankwell side is always silted up; during the building Thomas Telford had warned that the site was unsuitable, as the current would scour the foundations. The fine building on the other side of the river is Morris & Co.'s head office. It was built between 1919 and 1924 and cost around £30,000. The swing doors at the main entrance were made for an ocean liner, the interior is lined with oak panelling, and the staircase and stained-glass window in the lobby came from an old manor house at Church Preen. (*Abbeycolor*)

Above: The River Severn to Kingsland, 1963. The ice on the Quarry side of the river seems to have been broken into a channel, perhaps to free the pleasure boats moored close by before the ice became too thick and damaged them. On the opposite bank is Pengwern Boat Club. The club boathouse was designed by J.L. Randal and built in 1881 at a cost of £1,000. The building on the left at the top of the bank was built as a foundlings' hospital by Thomas Coram, in 1760, but this closed in 1774 through lack of funds. It became a prison for Dutch soldiers captured during the American War of Independence and was also used for a short while as a hospital during the rebuilding of the Salop Infirmary. In 1784 the corporation bought it as a workhouse. In 1882 Shrewsbury School moved here from their cramped site in the centre of town. The building to the right is the chapel. The first service was conducted there on 4 November 1883 when Bishop Walsham How preached the sermon. (*J. Savage*)

Opposite, top: The River Severn, 1962. This view was taken from the Porthill Bridge looking up stream towards the Welsh Bridge. The steps and pontoon are in front of the Boathouse Hotel garden. An old ferry took people across the river from that point for over 300 years until the Porthill Bridge was opened in 1922. The ice floes drifted down the river until they met an obstruction, usually a bridge, and compacted until there was a complete ice sheet covering the river. The river froze several times during the 1940s, '50s and '60s allowing skaters on to the river, but has not done so since the big freeze of 1981–2. (*J. Savage*)

Left: The River Severn to the Quarry, 1967. A blanket of thick snow covered the county town after a severe blizzard during the night of 8 December. The two pleasure boats were a familiar sight, taking visitors on trips up and down the river during the summer months of the 1960s. In the distance is an unusual view of the old Jubilee Baths and the new swimming pool standing side by side. The old baths were built to commemorate Queen Victoria's Golden Jubilee and were opened in 1894, while the new complex was officially opened in 1970. The long and short plunges from the old baths have been incorporated into the new centre. (*J. Savage*)

The Dingle, 31 January 1954. Whatever time of year you visit the Dingle it always retains its charm and beauty. Although the flowerbeds are covered by snow their outline can still be seen, and hardly a human footprint has spoilt this wonderful winter scene captured by photographer Jim Savage. The Dingle was one of the main areas where stone was quarried, giving the whole area its name. Towards the end of the nineteenth century the Dingle was landscaped, making it an attractive garden and a place protected from the harsher elements where the more delicate flowers and plants can survive and flourish, and where spring bulbs seem to appear sooner. (*J. Savage*)

The Quarry, *c.* 1955. In the booklet *Shrewsbury in Miniature*, printed in 1909, these landscaped gardens are described in this way: 'In the heart of the Quarry, lies the Dingle, which is, as it were, a bowl carved out of a massive emerald, and encrusted with gems. It was not wrought by Nature: it was dug out by men in search of stone, and from that fact the Quarry took its name.' The rock garden was built in 1924 by Elliott's of Stevenage and was a gift of the Horticultural Society, costing £693 12s 2d, while the fountain was given by the Odd Fellows. (*Author's Collection*)

The River Severn from Kingsland Bridge, *c.* 1963. This view is looking downstream towards the chimneys of Trouncer's Brewery in Longden Coleham. The Kingsland Bridge Co. was set up in 1872. The bridge is iron framed, has a 212 ft span and rests on stone piers. It cost in the region of £20,000 and was completed by 1881, but not opened until 28 July 1882, which coincided with the opening of the new Shrewsbury school. The bridge gave easy access to the school and the new leafy suburb of Kingsland. (*J. Savage*)

The approach road to Kingsland Bridge, February 1953. One of the officers of the Shropshire Fire Brigade inspects the damage to one of their appliances. The fire engine was taking a short cut from the fire station on Cross Hill to a fire in Longden Coleham. It came to grief after crossing the toll bridge and overturned as it rounded the first sharp bend leading towards Kennedy Road. The five firemen on board all escaped without serious injury although two of them, Harry Matthews and Len Buckley, were treated at the RSI for slight abrasions. The other crew on board were Sub-Officer George Thompson and Firemen Arthur Corfield and Charles Downes. A fire salvage lorry and cable were used to right the engine, and this was accomplished less than an hour after the crash. On the left with his hands on his hips is Sub-Officer George Thompson. (*J. Savage*)

The Quarry, *c.* 1955. This view of the Flower Show was taken from Beck's Fields. For a number of years after the old limes had been cut down, people unable to afford a ticket for the show would sit on this side of the river to view the horse jumping and other attractions in the main arena on the left and the high wire acts at the top of the bank. With the absence of the trees flagpoles were erected along the river walk and up the main avenue, and coloured lights were strung between them. During the 1953 show they hosted the National Show Jumping Championship, attracting such stars as Pat Smythe and Colonel Harry Llewellyn. (*Author's Collection*)

The Quarry, *c.* 1960. The stage show would attract huge crowds, no matter what the weather, to watch the performances of circus and music hall acts from all over the world. In the early years of the show eight hours of 'Marvellous Performances' were advertised with a fresh act every fifteen minutes. The performers included the Selbini Bicycle Troop, the Frantz Family, Lady and Gentlemen Acrobats in Full Evening Dress, Baretto and Artell, comical French Clowns and The Three Ottos, in Fun and Mischief. By the 1960s, however, with the advent of television and such shows as 'Sunday Night at the London Palladium', which could be watched from the comfort of an armchair, the stage's popularity waned and it was finally abandoned after nearly a hundred years. (*J. Savage*)

The River Severn, *c.* 1953. This sailing boat was used by youngsters from Shrewsbury school. They are turning in front of the Boathouse Hotel at the bottom of New Street. In 1900 the inn was owned by Southam's Brewery, had four private and five public rooms and a stable for one horse. During the 1930s it was run by the Abley family, who capitalised on its riverside location by running a large pleasure boat and keeping a fleet of rowing boats for hire. They also ran the Riverside Café at Shelton, where the pleasure boat and the rowers called for refreshment. The pleasure boat was called the *Lady Sue* after Mrs Abley. The inn kept a fleet of rowing boats until the middle of the 1960s when they were all washed away in a flood. (*J. Savage*)

The River Severn, 19 August 1958. This view was taken off the Grey Friar's Bridge looking upstream. The bridge was built to replace an old ferry linking Belle Vue and Coleham to the town and it was opened on 1 January 1880. The building on the left with the chimneys is Trouncer's Brewery, while the walk on the right is Victoria Avenue, laid out and planted with lime trees to commemorate one of Queen Victoria's Jubilees. The boys in the kayaks are Sea Scouts. Their headquarters was a room in Southam's brewery, but later they moved to the old mortuary on Smithfield Road. Ron James, a local Scout commissioner, took a great interest in the group and Mr Chester, a local schoolteacher who was assisted by Michael Sandford and Lloyd Hillman, led them in the 1950s. As well as kayaks they also had four large rowing boats, one for each patrol and each named after a sea bird. (*J. Savage*)

The River Severn, 17 July 1952. Just before Shrewsbury school break up for the summer holidays they hold the Bumping Races. They were started as a separate feature from the annual regatta in 1867 and were known as the inter-hall races. It is an inter-house competition held over several evenings, with each house fielding two or three boats. As well as the rowing the boys also run along the banks of the river urging their crew on to a greater effort. In the nineteenth century, after the bumping races had ended the crews would link their boats together, stand with their oars in the air and sing 'Hearts of Oak' and 'God Save the Queen'. Note the crowds of spectators on the Kingsland Bridge. (*J. Savage*)

The River Severn, *c.* 1955. The seats on the banks of the river opposite Shrewsbury school and Pengwern boathouses are always occupied during the summer months as people sit and watch the activities of the oarsmen on the water. Rowing was at first frowned on at Shrewsbury school, especially by Dr Butler, the headmaster from 1798 until 1836. Dr Kennedy succeeded him and under his leadership boating was allowed. Membership to the rowing club was restricted at first to boys above the fourth form who could pass a swimming test, and the first regatta was held in 1839. Money was raised to build a boathouse on the Isle of Poplars, opposite Coton Hill, but this never happened. At this time the small number of boats they had were kept at Evans's Boathouse on the site of their present boathouse. The larger of the two buildings on the opposite side of the river is the school's main boathouse. It was built in 1920 and was given to the school by Mr Pugh in memory of his son, J.E. Pugh, who was killed in the First World War. (*Author's Collection*)

The River Severn, 15 June 1958. The crowds are lining the banks of the river to watch the races at Pengwern Boat Club's annual regatta. In this race Loughborough on the left beat Ironbridge rowing club in the Junior Coxed Fours. At the 1963 regatta there were 112 crews competing in seventeen open events. Racing started at noon and finished at 7.05 p.m. At 8.30 p.m. all competitors were given free admission to the Boathouse Ball, which was celebrating the rebuilding of the clubroom, dance floor and bar. Non-competitors were charged 6s admission to the dance. The pontoon and boats on the right belong to George Cooper. He bought the business from Richard Ellis, and between them they hired out rowing boats to customers for over a hundred years. (*J. Savage*)

The Quarry, *c.* 1965. The go-ahead for the new £347,000 swimming pool and restaurant was given in November 1964 after four years of debate. The site for the new pool, which was to be a third of the size of an Olympic pool, has been cleared and the footings made ready. On the right the superintendent's house, occupied for so long by the Derbyshire family, and part of the old baths complex have been demolished. Under the distinctive dome roof was the pay kiosk, occupied for many years by Miss Derbyshire. During the 1950s children could stay in the swimming pool all day for just 6d! The building to the left of the dome is the old Long Plunge, which together with the Short Plunge has been incorporated into the new centre as the Claremont and Priory Pools. The new complex was opened to the public in December 1969, with its official opening taking place the following April. (*Abbeycolor*)

The River Severn, *c.* 1960. This area of the river is known as the Basin and is where the Rea Brook enters the Severn. The sand and gravel brought down by the current of the brook helped over the years to create the islands and the ford on which the English Bridge is built. The buildings on the right were on Carline Fields. They were demolished in the 1960s and the site was left open for several years, attracting parking and the odd fun fair. Modern apartments now occupy the site. The cottages to the left still survive but the Circular Office with the rounded roof and the white building next door have been demolished. The white house, known as Severn Villa, disappeared when the gyratory system was built, and the Circular Office was knocked down in 2001 for the building of Manser's bold but controversial antiques showroom. The Circular was established in about 1931 and was the Admag of the day, being issued every Friday priced 1*d.* (*Author's Collection*)

The River Severn, *c.* 1951. This photograph was taken just prior to the demolition of this bridge. It's the old Castle Walk Suspension Bridge, which was opened on Monday 7 November 1910 by the Mayor Councillor Blower. It connected the fast-growing suburb of Cherry Orchard to Castle Fields and gave a direct route into the centre of town. The bridge was constructed of steel wire; it was over 200 ft in length and cost just over £1,200. It replaced the Underdale Ferry that had run from a site just below the bridge for around forty years. In turn it was replaced by the country's first pre-stressed concrete cantilever bridge. (*Author's Collection*)

ACKNOWLEDGEMENTS

I would like to thank Simon Maiden of Abbeycolor for providing most of the prints for this volume from their vast collection of photographs of the 1960s. I would also like to thank Robert Evans, Abbeycolor's black and white expert, for turning the negatives into clear sharp prints. I am also grateful to Bronwen Brooks, John Bumford, Mr & Mrs Cowlishaw, the late Len Davies BEM, Mrs Dutton, A.A. Hector, Helen Jones, Mr King, David Laker, David Mitchell, Mrs Moden, Roy Pilsbury, John Pook, Ann Power, Dorothy Reynolds and Denis Sherwood for allowing me to use their photographs and to David Woodhouse for providing me with a great deal of ephemera from that period. I would also like to thank Joe and Charles Powell for their help with the railway photographs and the staff of the Shropshire Records and Research Centre for all their help, advice and expertise.

BIBLIOGRAPHY

Barker, J., *Shrewsbury Free Churches*, Brown & Brinnand, *c.* 1900.
Forrest, H.E., *The Old Houses of Shrewsbury*, Wilding & Son, 1920.
Hobbs, J.L., *Shrewsbury Street Names*, Wilding & Son, 1954.
Kelly's Directories of Shropshire, various dates.
Lloyd, L.C., *The Inns of Shrewsbury*, The Shrewsbury Circular, 1942.
Morriss, R.K., *Rail Centres: Shrewsbury*, Ian Allen Ltd, 1986.
Morriss, R.K. & Hoverd, K., *The Buildings of Shrewsbury*, Sutton, 1993.
Oldham, J.B., *A History of Shrewsbury School*, Basil Blackwell, 1952.
Riley, G., *The World's Wonder Show*, The Shropshire Horticultural Society, 1988.
Shrewsbury Advertiser, various dates.
Shrewsbury Chronicle, various dates.
Trinder, B., ed., *Victorian Shrewsbury*, Shropshire Libraries, 1984.
Ward, A.W., *The Bridges of Shrewsbury*, Wilding & Son, 1935.
Ward, A.W., *Shrewsbury, A Rich Heritage*, Wilding & Son, 1946.
West, J.M., *English Public Schools: Shrewsbury*, Blackie & Son Ltd, 1937.